MW00928272

A COMPREHENSIVE BORA BORA TRAVEL GUIDE BOOK 2024

The beauty of Bora Bora:

All you need to know, about traveling to Bora Bora in 2024

MASON WEST

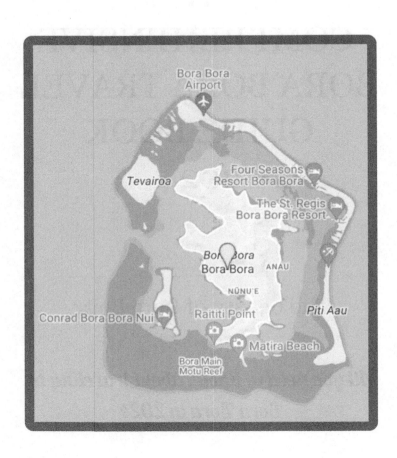

Copyright ©2023 by MASON WEST

All rights reserved. No part of this publication may be reproduced, distributed or transmitted in any form or by any means, including photocopying, recording ot other electronic or mechanical methods without the prior written permission of the publisher, except in the case of brief quotations embodied in critical reviews and certain other noncommercial uses permitted by copyright law.

CONTENTS

INTRODUCTION

Hush, traveler, and gather close. Let the trade winds whisper tales of a mythical island, born from fire and cradled by the ocean. This is Bora Bora, not just a postcard paradise, but a living legend etched in volcanic rock and shimmering lagoon waters.

Millions of years ago, a fiery dance began beneath the waves. Molten lava erupted, painting the sky with crimson hues and birthing a jagged peak from the ocean's depths. Mount Otemanu, they called it, the heart of the island, a sentinel watching over paradise.

Centuries melted into millennia, and Polynesian voyagers, guided by celestial whispers, arrived. They carved villages into the lush slopes, their laughter echoing through valleys draped in emerald. Legends bloomed alongside hibiscus flowers, stories of gods and heroes woven into the very fabric of this sacred land.

Time flowed like the gentle tide, washing away empires and etching new stories. Missionaries brought their faith, explorers mapped uncharted waters, and travelers, like you, sought solace in the island's embrace. Yet, through it all, Bora Bora's spirit remained, resilient and vibrant.

Today, we gather not to mourn, but to celebrate. For Bora Bora is not a relic of the past, but a living testament to its own story. The overwater bungalows, perched like elegant butterflies on the lagoon, whisper tales of luxury redefined. The coral reefs, bursting with life, sing of an ecosystem preserved. The smiles of the people, warm as the sun, echo the hospitality that has endured for centuries.

This is not just an island; it's a tapestry woven from fire, wind, and human spirit. It's a sanctuary for the soul, a playground for adventure, and a stage for timeless beauty. Yet, as we marvel at its perfection, remember: even paradise whispers stories of change.

So, tread lightly, dear traveler. Embrace the echoes of the past, celebrate the vibrant present, and leave only footprints of respect. For Bora Bora is not just a destination; it's a legacy we pass on, ensuring that its beauty continues to captivate hearts for generations to come.

This, then, is not an ending, but a new chapter. Turn the page, and embark on your own Bora Bora adventure, writing your own lines in the island's eternal story.

What Makes Bora Bora Unique

Forget the travel brochures – Bora Bora isn't just another pretty picture. It's a living legend, an island born from fire and cradled by the ocean, where turquoise waters and volcanic peaks create a world unlike any other. Here, luxury whispers tales of authenticity, adventure ignites the soul, and ancient traditions echo in every smile.

1. Where Fire Meets Paradise: Picture this: you hike lush slopes, feeling the volcanic hum of Mount Otemanu thrumming beneath your feet. This dramatic peak isn't just scenery; it's the island's heart, a silent guardian watching over paradise. Kayak through the lagoon, and its reflection dances on the water, reminding you of the fiery dance that birthed this magical land.

2. Whispers of Time: Polynesian voyagers weren't just explorers; they were storytellers. Dive into their vibrant dances, where pounding drums and graceful movements narrate tales of creation and ancestral wisdom. Learn ancient crafts like tapa cloth making, and feel the connection to a living history that stretches back centuries.

3. Luxury Redefined: Sure, overwater bungalows exist, but true Bora Bora luxury is beyond four walls. Imagine diving straight into the turquoise embrace from your private deck, surrounded by coral reefs teeming with life. Savor fresh seafood caught that morning, the island's bounty singing on your plate. As the sun paints the sky in fiery hues, sip a tropical cocktail, the trade winds whispering secrets in your ear.

4. Adventure Calling: Beyond the serenity, Bora Bora's soul pulses with adrenaline. Kayak through hidden coves, the only explorer to discover their untouched beauty. Hike Mount Pahia, and panoramic views unfurl like a map leading to endless possibilities. For the truly fearless, a jet ski safari awaits, the ocean spray and wind painting an unforgettable memory on your skin.

5. Hearts Open Wide: Forget tourist traps, Bora Bora is a community that welcomes you with open arms. Learn a few Tahitian phrases, and you'll unlock genuine smiles and heartwarming interactions. Witness their reverence for nature, their connection to their land, and gain a newfound appreciation for the delicate balance of this island paradise.

Bora Bora isn't just a destination; it's an experience that seeps into your soul. It's where fiery mountains meet turquoise dreams, where ancient echoes mingle with modern thrills, and where every traveler discovers their own unique piece of paradise. So, come, lose yourself in the magic, and unlock a chapter in your own story that will forever shimmer with the allure of Bora Bora.

PLANNING YOUR TRIP

Choosing the Right Time to Visit

Alright, adventurer, you've caught the Bora Bora bug (no, it's not contagious, but the wanderlust definitely is!). Now comes the fun part: planning your escape to paradise. But hold your coconuts, choosing the right time to visit requires more than just flipping a calendar (although, let's be honest, any day in Bora Bora is a good day). Fear not, intrepid traveler, for I shall be your guide through the jungle of seasons and weather patterns, ensuring your Bora Bora experience is anything but "meh."

First things first, let's dispel the myth: there's no "bad" time to visit Bora Bora. Yes, you read that right. This island goddess flaunts sunshine year-round, with temperatures that would make an iguana blush (in a good way, of course). So, what truly matters is aligning your visit with your own travel desires and, let's face it, budget.

Craving Sun-Kissed Perfection? Aim for the dry season (May to October). Think endless blue skies, balmy breezes, and enough sunshine to make even the grumpiest troll do a happy dance. Just be prepared to share paradise with fellow sun seekers, as this is peak season with prices reflecting its popularity.

Budget Traveler on a Mission? Consider the shoulder seasons (April and November). The crowds thin out, the prices mellow (think "spa treatment, not private island" mellow), and the weather remains gloriously sunny with occasional refreshing rain showers (perfect for washing away any lingering jet lag).

Adventure Junkie Seeking Serenity? The wet season (December to March) might be your jam. Picture lush landscapes glistening with tropical rain, fewer crowds, and the chance to score some sweet deals. Just be prepared for occasional downpours that can sometimes disrupt outdoor activities. But hey, who needs a fancy excursion when you can have a spontaneous mud mask courtesy of Mother Nature? Plus, the underwater world explodes with vibrant life during this season, making it a snorkeler's paradise.

Bonus Tip: Don't forget to factor in special events! The Heiva i Bora Bora festival in July explodes with vibrant dance, traditional crafts, and enough energy to power a small village. Or, witness the awe-inspiring Hawaiki Nui Va'a long-distance canoe race in November, where warriors of the ocean battle it out in a display of strength and cultural pride.

Remember, the "best" time to visit Bora Bora is the time that best suits your unique desires and budget. So, grab your metaphorical compass, set your priorities straight, and get ready to embark on an unforgettable adventure! Just one last thing: pack your sense of humor, because paradise has a way of throwing unexpected curveballs (think rogue coconuts or surprise rain showers). Embrace the chaos, laugh it off, and let Bora Bora weave its magic on your soul.

Visa and Entry Requirements

Hold onto your passports, paradise seekers! Before you sashay into the turquoise waters of Bora Bora, let's navigate the sometimes-confusing world of visas and entry requirements. Fear not, intrepid adventurers, for this guide will equip you with the knowledge to waltz past immigration with confidence (and minimal paperwork!).

Free Visa Fanfare: If you hail from one of these lucky nations, you can skip the visa hassle and enjoy visa-free entry to Bora Bora for up to 90 days:
• European Union: All member states
• Schengen Area: Iceland, Liechtenstein, Norway, Switzerland
• Andorra, Monaco, San Marino
• Argentina, Brazil, Chile, Uruguay
• Australia, New Zealand
• Canada, USA
• Fiji, Kiribati, Marshall Islands, Micronesia, Nauru, Palau, Papua New Guinea, Samoa, Solomon Islands, Tonga, Tuvalu, Vanuatu
• Hong Kong, Macao
• Japan, South Korea
• Malaysia, Singapore
• Mauritius, Seychelles
• United Arab Emirates

Visa Required, But Fear Not: Don't fret if your passport isn't on the list above! Obtaining a visa for Bora Bora is usually a straightforward process. You can apply online or at your nearest French embassy or consulate. Just remember, processing times can vary, so plan ahead to avoid any last-minute scrambles.

Universal Essentials: Visa-free or not, these items are your immigration must-haves:

• **Valid Passport:** Your gateway to island bliss, ensure it has at least 6 months validity remaining from your arrival date.

• **Proof of Onward/Return Travel:** Airlines might ask for this, so have your flight itinerary or booking confirmation handy.

• **Accommodation Booking:** Show immigration you have a place to rest your weary head (no couch surfing allowed!).

• **Sufficient Funds:** While not officially required, demonstrating you have enough money for your stay can prevent unnecessary inquiries.

Remember: While this guide provides a general overview, visa and entry requirements can change. Always double-check with the official website of the French Ministry of Foreign Affairs for the latest updates and specific requirements for your nationality. Don't rely solely on outdated information.

Budgeting for Your Bora Bora Adventure

Let's be honest, paradise doesn't come cheap, right? Fear not, budget-conscious adventurers! With a little planning and savvy tips, you can experience the magic of Bora Bora without breaking the bank. Buckle up, because we're diving into the world of Bora Bora budgeting!

First things first, set your priorities: What are your must-haves? Overwater bungalow or charming beachside fare? Snorkeling excursions or relaxing on the beach? Knowing what truly matters to you will help you allocate your funds effectively.

Accommodation: This is usually the biggest chunk of your budget. While overwater bungalows are the epitome of Bora Bora luxury, they come with a hefty price tag. **Consider:**
* **Beachfront bungalows:** Less expensive than overwater, often with stunning views and direct beach access.
* **Island guesthouses:** Immerse yourself in local culture with homestays or family-run guesthouses.
* **Vacation rentals:** Share a villa with friends or family for a cost-effective group trip.

Flights: Be flexible with travel dates and consider flying during the shoulder seasons (April & November) for better deals. Compare prices across airlines and booking platforms to snag the best fares.

Activities: Free options abound! Hike Mount Pahia for panoramic views, explore hidden coves by kayak, or snorkel straight from the beach. For paid activities, research and compare costs beforehand. Look for package deals or multi-day passes for discounts.

Food: Dining out can be pricey, but there are ways to save:
* **Self-cater:** Some accommodations have kitchens, or stock up on snacks and groceries from local markets.
* **Street food:** Sample delicious local fare from food trucks or stalls for a budget-friendly and authentic experience.
* **Happy hours:** Many restaurants offer discounted drinks and appetizers during happy hour.
* **Transportation:** Renting a bike or scooter is a fun and affordable way to explore the island. Public buses are also an option. Taxis can be expensive, so use them sparingly.

Remember:
• **Factor in hidden costs:** Airport transfers, taxes, tips, and travel insurance add up.
• **Consider travel deals and packages:** Look for bundled airfare, accommodation, and activity deals.
• **Embrace local experiences:** Free and budget-friendly options can be just as rewarding as pricey excursions.
• **Set realistic expectations:** Luxury comes at a premium, but paradise can be enjoyed on any budget.

With smart planning and a bit of resourcefulness, you can create a Bora Bora adventure that fits your wallet and fuels your wanderlust. Remember, the most valuable souvenirs are the memories you create, not the amount you spend. So, pack your sense of adventure, embrace the Bora Bora spirit, and get ready for an unforgettable experience!

Packing Essentials

Forget the endless "what-ifs" and start picturing yourself sinking your toes into Bora Bora's powdery sand. Yes, paradise awaits, but before you jet-set off, let's ensure your luggage isn't filled with "wish I'd packed that" regrets. This isn't your average packing list – it's a humorous survival guide to ensure you return from Bora Bora with memories (and tan lines) to brag about, not packing faux pas.

Sun Essentials

- **Sunscreen:** Remember, even Polynesian gods get sunburnt. Pack a reef-safe, SPF 30+ sunscreen and reapply religiously. Think of it as a love letter to your skin (and the coral reefs!).
- **Sunhat:** Picture this: you, looking effortlessly chic with a wide-brimmed hat shielding your face from the tropical sun. Bonus points for one that doubles as a fan for those "is-this-real-life?" moments.
- **Sunglasses:** Forget fashion statements, go for function first. Polarized shades that block harmful rays are your eyes' best friends (and make you look mysteriously cool, too).

Beach Essentials

- **Swimsuit (or two, or three):** This one's a no-brainer. Opt for quick-drying fabrics because let's face it, nobody wants to be the "damp swimsuit" person. Remember, confidence is the best accessory, so rock whatever makes you feel like a beach goddess (or god)!
- **Beach towel:** Unless you fancy sandcastles as clothing, pack a beach towel. Bonus points for one

with a hilarious island-themed design to spark conversations (and laughter).

• **Water shoes:** Coral doesn't play nice with bare feet. Protect your precious digits with water shoes – think of them as tiny underwater shoes of invincibility!

Clothing

• **Breathable, light layers:** Think linen shirts that billow dramatically in the breeze and flowy dresses that make you feel like you're in a rom-com. Comfort is key, so ditch the stiff jeans and embrace island life.

• **Walking shoes:** Exploring hidden coves and charming villages deserves comfortable footwear. Remember, blisters and stunning scenery don't make a good combo.

• **One "fancy" outfit:** Pack something nice for a special dinner or to impress the locals with your impeccable island fashion sense. Remember, even paradise deserves a touch of elegance (even if it's just borrowed).

Other Must-Haves

• **Quick-drying travel adapter:** Don't get caught with a dead phone and a million photo ops. Pack a travel adapter to keep your electronics juiced and ready to capture every magical moment.

- **Reusable water bottle:** Stay hydrated and eco-friendly with a reusable water bottle. Plus, it gives you an excuse to refill at charming cafes and chat with the locals (hydration AND cultural immersion – win-win!).
- **Dry bag:** Picture this: you're on a boat trip, camera in hand, capturing the perfect sunset...oops, rogue wave! A dry bag saves the day (and your electronics).
- **First-aid kit:** Be prepared for minor scrapes, insect bites, or the occasional "coconut incident" (yes, they happen!). Pack a small first-aid kit for peace of mind (and to avoid exorbitant pharmacy bills).
- **Entertainment:** Flights and downtime happen. Pack a book, journal, or even a deck of cards to keep boredom at bay. Who knows, you might even strike up a friendly game with a fellow traveler.

Bonus Tip: Pack a light backpack or tote for day trips. It'll hold your essentials and free your hands for important things, like snapping selfies with manta rays or sipping mai tais.

Remember, this is just a starting point. Tailor it to your activities and personality. Most importantly, pack your sense of adventure, a dash of humor, and an open mind. Bora Bora awaits, and with the right essentials, you're guaranteed an unforgettable adventure!

GETTING THERE

Flights to Bora Bora

First-time Bora Bora adventurer? Buckle up, because this guide equips you with all the details you need to navigate the skies and land in island paradise! We'll cover both direct and island-hopping options, complete with estimated prices, baggage fees, and insider tips for a smooth journey.

Direct Delight: Luxury with a Price Tag

Craving a seamless arrival straight into Bora Bora's embrace? Direct flights offer ultimate convenience, but be prepared for a higher price tag. Here's the breakdown:

Airlines:
* **Air Tahiti Nui:** The primary player, offering direct flights from Los Angeles (LAX) and San Francisco (SFO) with starting prices around $2,500+ (roundtrip). Expect higher prices from other cities like New York or Paris.
* **Air France**: Offers some direct flights from Paris (CDG) at premium prices.
* **Flight Time:** Approximately 8-10 hours from the West Coast, 20+ hours from Europe.

Baggage Fees:
• Air Tahiti Nui usually includes one checked bag (23kg) in their Economy fares. Additional checked bags range from $100-$200 each. Carry-on allowance is one personal item and one standard cabin bag (12kg).
• Air France baggage fees vary depending on route and booking class. Expect to pay around $100-$200 for an additional checked bag and $50-$100 for a carry-on exceeding their standard allowance.

• **Pros:** Seamless journey, comfortable seating, Polynesian hospitality onboard.
• **Cons:** Most expensive option, limited departure cities, less flexibility with dates.

Island Hopper: Adventure & Savings
Embrace the island spirit and combine adventure with budget-friendly fares! Fly into Tahiti's Faa'a International Airport (PPT) and connect to Bora Bora with Air Tahiti.

Airlines:
• **Air Tahiti:** Operates connecting flights from PPT to Bora Bora (BOB) with fares starting around

$500-$800+ (roundtrip). Prices depend on seasonality and demand.
• **Flight Time:** Approximately 50 minutes from PPT to BOB, plus flight time to PPT from your origin city (usually longer than direct flights).

Baggage Fees:
Air Tahiti generally includes one checked bag (23kg) in their Economy fares. Additional checked bags range from $75-$150 each. Carry-on allowance is one personal item and one standard cabin bag (12kg).

• **Pros:** Budget-friendly, experience multiple islands, shorter connecting flight compared to some island-hopping routes.
• **Cons:** Longer overall travel time, layovers in Tahiti (potential for delays), less legroom on smaller connecting aircraft.

Pro Tips for First-Timers:
• **Book Early:** Secure your tickets 3-6 months in advance, especially during peak season (May-Oct).
• **Compare Prices:** Check Google Flights, Kayak, airline websites, and travel agencies. Flexibility with dates can help score deals.
• **Mind Baggage:** Pack light and review airline baggage allowances/fees to avoid surprise charges.

- **Embrace Layovers:** Turn your Tahiti layover into an adventure! Explore Papeete, relax on a beach, or even book a day trip to another island.
- **Shoulder Seasons:** Consider April & November for potentially better deals.

Remember: Prices are approximate and can fluctuate. Double-check official airline websites for the latest fares and baggage information before booking.

Bonus Tip: Pack a light backpack for your layover or connecting flight. Store essentials like snacks, water, and entertainment, keeping you comfortable and prepared for any adventure.

With this detailed guide and some planning, you'll be soaring towards Bora Bora like a seasoned traveler.

Airport and Transportation

Picture this: you step off the plane, greeted by Bora Bora's intoxicating blend of turquoise waters, lush greenery, and balmy air. But before diving into island bliss, let's navigate the arrival logistics. This guide tackles Bora Bora Motu Mute Airport (BOB) and your onward journey, ensuring a smooth transition from sky to paradise, complete with approximate prices and fees to help you plan your budget.

Touching Down at Motu Mute Airport:
Motu Mute Airport is small and charming, offering a quick and efficient disembarkation process. Collect your passport and baggage claim tickets before exiting the arrival hall. Remember to check visa requirements for your nationality; you can usually find this information on your embassy or consulate's website.

Visa Requirements:
Most nationalities don't require visas for stays under 90 days, but double-check with your embassy or the nearest French consulate for any updates.

Currency Exchange:
While currency exchange booths are available at the airport, rates might be less favorable. Consider exchanging some money beforehand or using ATMs in the arrival hall for potentially better rates.

ACCOMMODATIONS

Luxurious Resorts

Forget cookie-cutter hotels – in Bora Bora, accommodations become immersive havens, whispering promises of turquoise horizons and unparalleled luxury. Imagine waking up to a harmony of waves lapping against your private plunge pool, gazing out at coral reefs teeming with life, and indulging in world-class spas and gourmet feasts. Dive into this guide to Bora Bora's luxurious resorts, where each night feels like a dream, complete with names, approximate prices, and insider tips to craft your bespoke island escape:

Overwater Bungalows
• **The epitome of Bora Bora living:** Picture yourself ensconced in a thatched-roof bungalow at the Four Seasons Resort Bora Bora. Imagine diving straight into the crystal-clear lagoon from your private deck, infinity pool shimmering beside you. Expect unparalleled service, exquisite dining, and breathtaking views – starting around $1,500 per night, but trust us, it's worth every penny. The Four Seasons Resort Bora Bora is situated on the island of Bora Bora in the Society Islands of French

Polynesia, accessible from Bora Bora Airport by a short 15 to 20-minute boat ride.

• **Seclusion meets indulgence at the Conrad Bora Bora Nui.** Imagine stepping off your bungalow into a hidden cove, turquoise waters lapping at your doorstep. Unwind in your private plunge pool, savor gourmet delights in your overwater villa, and soak in the serenity of your own slice of paradise. Prices start around $1,200 per night, and the memories will last a lifetime. The Conrad Bora Bora Nui is situated on the Motu To'opua island, an islet off the coast of Bora Bora in French Polynesia. Accessible from Bora Bora Airport, the resort can be reached through a scenic boat transfer lasting approximately 15 to 20 minutes.

Beachfront Villas:

•**Indulge in barefoot luxury at the InterContinental Bora Bora Resort & Thalasso Spa.** Imagine sprawling beachfront villas nestled along pristine white sand, your private garden a gateway to the turquoise embrace of the ocean. Pamper yourself at the renowned Deep Ocean Spa, indulge in delectable Polynesian cuisine, and create memories that shimmer brighter than the lagoon – all for around $800 per night. The InterContinental Bora Bora Resort & Thalasso

Spa is on Motu Piti Aau, Bora Bora. You can reach it by pre-arranged resort boat transfer from the airport, taking about 30 minutes.

• **Embrace the romance at the St. Regis Bora Bora Resort.** Imagine sunrise dips in your infinity pool overlooking the majestic Mount Otemanu, followed by decadent breakfasts on your private terrace. Explore the vibrant coral reefs teeming with life, and be swept away by the unparalleled service and exquisite Polynesian ambiance. Prices start around $1,000 per night, but the experience is priceless. The St. Regis Bora Bora Resort is located on Motu piti A, Bora Bora. Guests typically pre-arrange a private boat transfer from the airport, which takes approximately 15 minutes.

Motu Retreats:

• **Imagine having your own private island at Le Taha'a by Pearl Resorts.** Imagine a secluded motu (islet) where only the gentle whisper of waves and the rustle of palm trees disturb your serenity. Enjoy personalized service, indulge in fresh seafood feasts under the starlit sky, and embrace the unparalleled exclusivity – starting around $5,000 per night, an investment in an unforgettable experience. Le Taha'a by Pearl Resorts is nestled on a private motu (islet) off the east coast of Taha'a,

French Polynesia. It's a 35-minute boat ride from Raiatea Airport and a 5-minute boat ride from the village of Tapuamu. You can also opt for a breathtaking 14-minute helicopter flight from Bora Bora for stunning aerial views.

• **Discover ultimate seclusion at the Brando Marlon Brando Resort.** Imagine stepping onto your private motu, named after the legendary actor who dreamt it into existence. Bask in the untouched beauty of this eco-haven, snorkel through coral gardens teeming with life, and create memories that whisper of paradise itself. Prices start around $7,000 per night, but for a once-in-a-lifetime escape, it's a dream worth pursuing. The Brando resort, on Marlon Brando's private Tetiaroa atoll, French Polynesia, requires a 45-minute private plane flight from Tahiti or helicopter transfers from other islands

Pro Tips:
• **Book early:** These havens fill up fast, especially during peak season (May-Oct). Secure your dream accommodation 3-6 months in advance.
• **Consider all-inclusive options:** Some resorts offer packages covering meals, drinks, and activities, potentially providing better value for money.

- **Compare offerings:** Each resort boasts unique experiences and amenities. Research thoroughly to find the perfect fit for your desires and budget.

Factor in additional fees: Resort fees, taxes, and gratuities can add up. Make sure to carefully go through the details before making a reservation to prevent unexpected surprises.

Insider Tip: Look for special packages or promotions, particularly during shoulder seasons (April & November), when you might snag luxurious accommodations at better rates.

Romance under the Stars:

- **Sofitel Kia Ora Moorea:** Imagine a secluded haven on its own private motu, accessible only by boat. At Sofitel Kia Ora Moorea Private Island, luxurious bungalows with private plunge pools dot the shoreline, each framed by swaying palm trees and breathtaking ocean views. Savor gourmet delights under the starlit sky, indulge in rejuvenating spa treatments, and experience the magic of a truly private paradise. Prices start around $1,000 per night, an investment in an unforgettable romantic escape.
- **Pearl Beach Resort & Spa:** Escape to an intimate haven nestled on a secluded cove at Pearl Beach Resort & Spa. Enjoy spacious bungalows with

private decks overlooking the lagoon, where the gentle rhythm of waves serenades you to sleep. Unwind at the renowned Deep Nature Spa, indulge in delectable Polynesian cuisine, and explore hidden coves with personalized guidance from the attentive staff. Prices start around $700 per night, offering a blend of luxury and intimacy perfect for rekindling romance.

Eco-Conscious Retreat:

• **Fare Te Are Nui:** Embrace sustainable luxury at Fare Te Are Nui, an eco-conscious haven nestled amongst lush gardens. Built with local materials and powered by renewable energy, your private bungalow blends seamlessly with the surrounding environment. Enjoy locally sourced cuisine, participate in cultural experiences like weaving workshops, and explore the island's natural beauty with a guided eco-tour. Prices start around $350 per night, making it an ideal choice for eco-conscious travelers seeking a meaningful island escape.

• **Villa Mahana:** Immerse yourself in the natural beauty of Bora Bora at Villa Mahana, where traditional Polynesian architecture meets modern comforts. Enjoy spacious bungalows with private balconies overlooking the lagoon, surrounded by lush gardens teeming with tropical birds. Relax by the infinity pool, savor fresh seafood dishes at the beachfront restaurant, and explore the island's underwater wonders with knowledgeable dive guides. Prices start around $600 per night, offering a balance of comfort, sustainability, and authentic island experiences.

Pro Tips:
• Boutique hotels often fill up quickly. Secure your haven 3-6 months in advance, especially during peak season (May-Oct).
• Consider smaller, family-run establishments for a truly personalized experience.
• Seize the chance to engage with locals and gain insights into their cultural heritage.
• Pack light and eco-friendly items, respecting the island's fragile environment.

Remember, a boutique hotel experience is about immersing yourself in the unique spirit of Bora Bora. So, let go of expectations, embrace the island's rhythm, and get ready to discover hidden gems and create memories that will forever shimmer with the magic of paradise.

Budget-Friendly Options

Bora Bora whispers promises of turquoise waters and white-sand beaches, but whispers don't have to break the bank! Forget hefty price tags and discover the magic of this island paradise with these budget-friendly options:

Guesthouses & Family-Run Stays:
• **Raihei Location:** Immerse yourself in the heart of Vaitape village at Raihei Location. This family-run haven offers dorm beds (starting around $45 per night) and private rooms (around $90 per night) with a warm, local atmosphere. Enjoy home-cooked meals, mingle with friendly locals, and experience authentic island life at its finest. Located in Vaitape village, the main village on Bora Bora.
• **Sunset Hill Lodge:** Embrace panoramic lagoon views and laid-back island vibes at Sunset Hill Lodge. Studios and apartments, all with kitchenettes, start around $120 per night, offering great value for budget-conscious travelers. Relax by the pool, borrow kayaks to explore the lagoon, and enjoy stunning sunsets from your balcony. Located on the hills overlooking Matira Point, offering incredible views.

- **Pension Temaeva:** Experience Polynesian hospitality at Pension Temaeva, located steps away from Matira Beach. Simple yet comfortable rooms with shared bathrooms start around $70 per night, offering an affordable option for beach lovers. Snorkel right off the beach, enjoy local food at nearby restaurants, and soak up the sun-kissed atmosphere. Located on Matira Point, known for its beautiful beach and calm waters.

Hostels & Camping:

- **Maitiki Island Youth Hostel**: Mingle with fellow travelers and enjoy the social vibe at Maitiki Island Youth Hostel. Dorm beds start around $35 per night, making it an ideal option for solo adventurers or budget-minded groups. Participate in organized activities like snorkeling trips and cultural experiences, and discover the island together. Located on Motu Mute, the main island where the airport is situated.
- **Camping:** Embark on a rustic adventure with camping options on Bora Bora's main island and motus. Public campsites (around $10 per night) offer basic amenities like toilets and showers, while private motu campsites (around $50 per night) provide more privacy and seclusion. Remember to bring your own camping gear and be prepared for a truly immersive island experience. Public campsites

can be found on Motu Mute and Motu Tapu, while private motu campsites are scattered across various islets.

Pro Tips:
• Travel during shoulder seasons (April & November) for better deals on accommodation and activities.
• Consider cooking some meals yourself – grocery stores offer affordable options compared to restaurant dining.
• Take advantage of free activities like hiking, exploring villages, and swimming in the lagoon.
• Look for package deals that combine accommodation with activities for potential savings.

The true magic of Bora Bora lies beyond luxury. Embrace the simple pleasures, connect with the locals, and discover the island's authentic charm within your budget.

EXPLORING BORA BORA

Top Attractions

Forget the map, ditch the itinerary – in Bora Bora, exploration is an intoxicating blend of adventure and awe. Imagine kayaking over turquoise waters, feeling the spray tickle your face as you discover hidden coves. Picture scaling Mount Otemanu, reaching the peak for panoramic views that steal your breath. Dive into this quick guide to Bora Bora's top attractions, ready to ignite your island exploration:

Jewel of the Lagoon:

1 **Snorkeling & Diving:** Glide amidst vibrant coral reefs teeming with exotic fish, playful dolphins, and majestic manta rays. Witness the underwater magic with:

• **Topcat Bora Bora:** Snorkeling tours start around $80 per person, diving excursions from $150 per person.

• **Bora Bora Blue No Limit:** Offers guided dives for all levels, prices starting around $180 per person.

- **Top Dive:** Renowned for eco-friendly diving experiences, tours from $200 per person.

2 Land Ahoy!
- **Mount Otemanu:** Hike or 4x4 your way to the island's heart, the mighty Mount Otemanu. Lush valleys unfurl beneath you, the iconic peak piercing the sky – a sight that will leave you speechless.
- **Aruri Mountain Tour:** Guided hikes start around $120 per person, including transportation and local insights.
- **Polynesian ATV:** Explore by 4x4, tours from $200 per person, offering breathtaking viewpoints and cultural stops.

3 Island Hopping
- **Motu Magic:** Embark on a private boat tour, island hopping to secluded motus (islets). Pristine beaches beckon, swaying palm trees whisper secrets, and crystal-clear waters invite you to dive in. Create memories that shimmer brighter than the lagoon itself.
- **Captain Miki Lagoon Tours:** Personalized boat tours to various motus, starting around $300 per person (minimum 2 pax).
- **Bora Bora Lagoon Service:** Explore private motus for picnics, snorkeling, or relaxation, tours from $250 per person (minimum 4 pax).

4 Sunset Symphony

• **Lagoon Cruise:** As the sun dips below the horizon, painting the sky in fiery hues, set sail on a romantic lagoon cruise. Savor delectable bites, sip tropical cocktails, and let the island's beauty wash over you – pure bliss!

• **Bora Bora Pearl Cruises:** Sunset cruises with dinner and open bar, starting around $200 per person.

• **Matira Beachcomber:** Traditional Polynesian outrigger canoe sunset cruises, from $150 per person.

Insider Tip: Pack your sense of adventure, a camera to capture the magic, and an open heart to embrace the island's soul. Bora Bora's true treasures lie beyond the guidebooks – waiting for you to discover them!

Remember, these are just starting prices, and rates can vary depending on group size, season, and specific inclusions. Do your research and compare options to find the perfect fit for your budget and desired experience.

Outdoor Activities

Forget the gym treadmill, trade it for Bora Bora's turquoise playground! Imagine jet skiing across the lagoon, the wind whipping through your hair as you chase the setting sun. Picture paddling a traditional outrigger canoe, feeling the rhythm of the waves carrying you to hidden coves. Dive into this guide to Bora Bora's outdoor adventures, ready to unleash your inner explorer:

Adrenaline Rush

• **Jet Skiing:** Feel the exhilaration as you carve through the lagoon, volcanic peaks your backdrop, chasing dolphins or exploring secluded motus. Remember, life jackets and licenses are mandatory! (Rental prices start around $100-$150 per hour)

• **Parasailing:** Soar high above the lagoon, the turquoise canvas stretching beneath you as you soak in panoramic views of Mount Otemanu and beyond. (Expect prices around $80-$120 per person)

• **Shark & Ray Feeding:** Embark on a thrilling encounter with nature's gentle giants. Observe blacktip reef sharks and majestic stingrays as they glide gracefully around you in their natural habitat. (Tours typically range from $150-$200 per person)

Island Explorer

• **Stand-Up Paddleboarding (SUP):** Glide across the glassy waters, feeling the gentle sway of the waves as you explore hidden coves, mangrove forests, and coral reefs teeming with life. Rentals start around $20-$30 per hour.

• **Kayaking:** Embark on a peaceful adventure, paddling along the coastline, discovering secluded beaches and hidden gems. Kayak rentals start around $30-$40 per day.

• **Hiking:** Lace up your boots and conquer diverse trails. Hike the lush slopes of Mount Otemanu for breathtaking views, or explore ancient Polynesian marae (temples) hidden within the island's interior. Guided tours range from $50-$80 per person.

Underwater World

• **Scuba Diving:** Dive into a kaleidoscope of colors, exploring vibrant coral reefs teeming with exotic fish, playful dolphins, and majestic manta rays. Discover underwater shipwrecks and hidden underwater caves. Diving excursions start around $150-$200 per person.

• **Snorkeling:** Float effortlessly amidst vibrant coral reefs, surrounded by schools of colorful fish. Witness the underwater magic without the commitment of scuba diving. Snorkeling tours start around $80-$120 per person.

• **Insider Tip:** Consider all-inclusive resorts that often offer complimentary water sports equipment like kayaks and paddleboards. Look for local operators specializing in specific activities for personalized experiences and insider knowledge.

Remember, safety first! Always check weather conditions, follow your guide's instructions, and respect the island's environment.

Cultural Experiences

Bora Bora's magic goes beyond the turquoise waters and breathtaking scenery. It's the vibrant culture, steeped in ancient traditions and Polynesian warmth, that truly captivates the heart. Dive into this guide and unlock authentic experiences that will leave you enriched and forever connected to the island's soul

Journey Through Time

• **Visit a Marae:** Explore ancient Polynesian temples (marae), silent testaments to the island's rich history and spiritual heritage. Learn about the significance of these sacred sites and feel the energy of generations past. (Entrance fees vary, typically around $5-$10 per person)

• **Attend a Traditional Ceremony:** Witness the captivating beauty of a Hura Tahitian dance performance, the dancers' vibrant costumes and mesmerizing movements telling stories of the island's folklore and legends. (Shows are often held at resorts or cultural centers, prices vary)

• **Discover Local Crafts:** Immerse yourself in the vibrant art scene. Browse through local markets overflowing with hand-woven baskets, intricate wood carvings, and colorful pareos (sarongs). Support local artisans and take home a piece of Bora Bora's cultural heritage. (Prices vary depending on the craft and artist)

Culinary Delights

• **Indulge in a Polynesian Feast:** Savor the island's unique flavors at a traditional "ma'a Tahiti" feast. Sample fresh seafood cooked in an underground oven, succulent meats marinated in tropical spices, and delectable local fruits. (Prices vary depending on the restaurant and inclusions)

• **Learn to Cook Like a Local:** Take a cooking class and unlock the secrets of Polynesian cuisine. Learn to prepare traditional dishes like poisson cru (marinated raw fish) and po'e (a sweet pudding), and impress your friends back home with your newfound skills. (Cooking classes typically range from $50-$100 per person)

• **Visit a Local Farm:** Embark on a farm tour and witness firsthand the island's agricultural practices. Learn about the importance of local produce in the Polynesian diet and sample fresh fruits and vegetables straight from the source. (Farm tour prices vary depending on the operator)

Connecting with the Community

• **Attend a Village Festival:** Immerse yourself in the vibrant energy of a local festival. Witness traditional dance performances, participate in games, and savor delicious food, all while connecting with the friendly island community. (Festivals are held throughout the year, check local listings for dates and locations)

• **Learn a Few Tahitian Phrases:** Go beyond "mauruuru" (thank you)! Learn basic Tahitian phrases to greet locals, order food, and have simple conversations. This small effort shows respect for their culture and opens doors to deeper connections.

• **Support Local Initiatives:** Give back to the island by supporting local businesses and initiatives. Purchase souvenirs from local artisans, donate to environmental conservation projects, or volunteer your time at a community center.

Insider Tip: Embrace the spirit of "maeva" (welcome) and approach cultural experiences with an open mind and respectful heart. Ask questions, participate actively, and appreciate the unique traditions that make Bora Bora so special.

Remember, cultural experiences are not just about ticking things off a list. They're about forging connections, understanding a different way of life, and enriching your own journey. So, step outside your comfort zone, embrace the island's cultural tapestry, and create memories that resonate far beyond the souvenir pareo.

Local Cuisine and Dining

Forget generic meals, Bora Bora's cuisine is a colorful scope of fresh, local ingredients, Polynesian traditions, and French flair. Dive into a flavor-filled joyride, sending your taste buds on a rollercoaster of delight with these dishes that are practically begging to be devoured:

Local Specialties:
• **Poisson Cru:** This vibrant appetizer features raw fish (tuna, mahi-mahi, or lobster) marinated in coconut milk, lime juice, and local spices. Expect to pay around $20-$30 per serving at most

restaurants. Find it almost everywhere, from beach shacks to fine-dining establishments.

• **Ahimaa:** Experience the traditional "ahimaa" feast. Tender meats, seafood, and vegetables slow-cooked in an underground oven for an earthy, smoky flavor. Prices vary depending on the restaurant and portion size, ranging from $40-$70 per person. Try Matira Beachcomber for an authentic experience.

• **Fruits de Mer:** Indulge in fresh seafood platters featuring grilled lobster (around $80-$120), pan-seared scallops ($40-$60), or local "picots" (sea snails) cooked in coconut milk ($20-$30). Le Motu at InterContinental Bora Bora Resort & Thalasso Spa offers an excellent selection.

Beyond the Classics

• **Vanilla Delights:** Savor the unique flavor of Bora Bora's prized vanilla in creamy desserts like vanilla crème brûlée ($15-$20) or savory sauces like vanilla beurre blanc ($30-$40) for grilled fish. Try La Plage Restaurant at The St. Regis Bora Bora Resort for decadent options.

• **Rougail:** This spicy tomato-based condiment with chilies and onions adds a fiery kpick to grilled meats and fish. It's usually served complimentary with main courses at most restaurants.

- **Exotic Fruits:** Immerse yourself in the vibrant fruit selection. Enjoy juicy pineapples and sweet mangoes ($2-$5 each), or try exotic starfruit and tangy dragon fruit ($5-$10 each) at local markets or roadside stalls.

Romantic Dining Experiences

- **Sunset Cruises:** Sail into paradise on a private sunset cruise with a gourmet dinner onboard. Expect an intimate setting and delectable dishes for around $200-$300 per person. Many resorts offer this experience, or check with operators like Captain Miki Lagoon Tours.
- **Overwater Bungalows:** Many offer in-room dining, transforming your deck into a romantic haven. Savor a private chef-prepared meal under the stars for around $150-$250 per person, depending on the resort and menu.
- **Local Village Restaurants:** Immerse yourself in the island vibe at family-run eateries like Chez Hinano near Matira Beach. Sample local specialties for $20-$40 per person and enjoy warm hospitality.

Insider Tips

- Embrace the "slow food" philosophy – savor the experience, don't rush.
- Be adventurous – try new dishes and ask for recommendations.

• Seek restaurants using local ingredients for an authentic taste.
• Tipping is not customary, but a small gesture is appreciated.

With its diverse flavors and unforgettable settings, Bora Bora's culinary scene promises an adventure for your taste buds. So, grab a fork, embrace the island spirit, and get ready to be delighted!

Water Adventures

Snorkeling and Diving Spots
Bora Bora's turquoise waters and vibrant coral reefs beckon underwater explorers of all levels. Whether you're a seasoned diver seeking adrenaline-pumping encounters or a curious snorkeler wanting to peek into the kaleidoscope of life below, the island offers an unforgettable aquatic adventure. Let's dive into some of the top snorkeling and diving spots:

Snorkeling Delights:
• **The Coral Garden:** Aptly named, this shallow haven near Motu Pitiu boasts diverse coral formations teeming with colorful fish, stingrays, and playful clams. Perfect for families and beginners, it's easily accessible by kayak or boat tour.

- **Anau Inner Reef:** This calm lagoon area near the main island shelters an abundance of marine life. Glide alongside schools of butterflyfish, spot majestic stingrays, and even encounter blacktip reef sharks with experienced guides.
- **Matira Point:** The shallow waters off Matira Beach offer incredible underwater experiences. Witness vibrant coral formations teeming with clownfish, angelfish, and even eagle rays. Perfect for a relaxing snorkel after a day on the beach.
- **Coral Gardens Bora Bora:** Nestled near Motu Mute, this hidden gem boasts healthy coral formations and diverse marine life. Expect anemones hosting clownfish, schools of surgeonfish, and occasional sightings of turtles.

Diving for Thrill Seekers:

- **Teavanui Pass:** For experienced divers seeking an adrenaline rush, Teavanui Pass offers encounters with sharks, barracuda, and manta rays as they navigate the powerful currents. This drift dive requires advanced certifications and experienced guides.
- **Anau Outer Reef:** Dive deeper at Anau's outer reef wall, descending into a vibrant underwater world. Explore swim-throughs teeming with fish, encounter playful dolphins, and witness the majestic manta rays gliding gracefully by.

- **The Aquarium:** This deep dive site near Motu Tapu features unique coral formations, overhangs teeming with colorful fish, and even resident moray eels. It's a photographer's paradise, offering diverse subjects and stunning backdrops.
- **Tiputa Pass:** Renowned for its thrilling drift dives, Tiputa Pass boasts strong currents attracting hammerhead sharks, manta rays, and even humpback whales during migration season. Only for experienced divers with proper certification and guides.

Choosing Your Adventure:
- **Consider your experience level:** Opt for calm lagoon areas like the Coral Garden for beginners, while experienced divers can explore thrilling currents at Teavanui Pass.
- **Research dive operators:** Choose reputable companies with experienced guides familiar with local conditions and safety protocols.
- **Group or private tours:** Snorkeling tours are often offered in groups, while diving excursions can be private or shared, depending on your preference.
- **Conservation matters:** Choose eco-friendly operators committed to responsible practices and reef conservation.

Pro Tip: Pack reef-safe sunscreen and avoid touching coral formations to preserve this underwater paradise for future generations.

Snorkeling and diving offer a glimpse into the incredible underwater world of Bora Bora. With its diverse marine life and stunning coral reefs, an aquatic adventure here is an experience you'll never forget. Dive in and explore!

Overwater Excursions

Bora Bora's iconic overwater bungalows offer breathtaking views and luxurious comfort, but the true magic lies beyond your private deck. Embark on unforgettable excursions that delve deeper into the island's turquoise heart, creating memories that shimmer brighter than the lagoon itself:

Island Hopping Bliss:
• **Motu Magic:** Charter a private boat and explore the secluded motus (islets) scattered around Bora Bora. Snorkel in crystal-clear waters teeming with colorful fish, bask on pristine beaches, and enjoy delicious picnics under swaying palm trees. Prices start around $300 per person (minimum 2 pax), with operators like Captain Miki Lagoon Tours and

Bora Bora Lagoon Service offering personalized experiences.

• **Sunset Sandbar Escape:** Sail to a secluded sandbar as the sun dips below the horizon, painting the sky in fiery hues. Enjoy a romantic dinner, sip cocktails on the sand, and witness the island's beauty unfold before you. Expect prices around $200 per person with operators like Matira Beachcomber and Bora Bora Pearl Cruises offering these unique experiences.

• **Stingray & Shark Encounter:** Embark on a thrilling encounter with Bora Bora's gentle giants. Observe graceful stingrays gliding through the water, witness blacktip reef sharks in their natural habitat, and learn about the importance of these creatures in the ecosystem. Tours typically range from $150-$200 per person, with operators like Topcat Bora Bora and Bora Bora Blue No Limit specializing in these adventures.

Underwater Wonders:

• **Scuba Diving Adventures:** Explore vibrant coral reefs teeming with exotic fish, playful dolphins, and majestic manta rays. Discover underwater shipwrecks and hidden caves with operators like Top Dive and Bora Bora Blue No Limit, offering dives for all levels starting around $150 per person.

- **Snorkeling Exploration:** Glide effortlessly amidst vibrant coral reefs, surrounded by schools of colorful fish. Witness the underwater magic without the commitment of scuba diving. Snorkeling tours start around $80-$120 per person with operators like Topcat Bora Bora and Bora Bora Lagoon Service offering various options.
- **Jet Ski Adventures:** Feel the exhilaration as you carve through the lagoon, volcanic peaks your backdrop, chasing dolphins or exploring secluded motus. Remember, life jackets and licenses are mandatory! Rental prices start around $100-$150 per hour.

Romantic Rendezvous:

- **Sunset Cruise & Dinner:** Sail into paradise on a romantic sunset cruise with a gourmet dinner onboard. Savor delectable bites, sip tropical cocktails, and let the island's beauty wash over you – pure bliss! Prices start around $200 per person with operators like Bora Bora Pearl Cruises and Matira Beachcomber offering these unforgettable experiences.
- **Private Island Escape:** Rent a private motu for a day, enjoying complete seclusion with your loved one. Swim in your own private lagoon, sunbathe on pristine sand, and indulge in a picnic prepared by your resort or a local caterer. Prices vary depending

on the motu size and amenities, but expect to start around $500 for the day.

Pro Tip: Consider all-inclusive resorts that often offer complimentary water sports equipment like kayaks and paddleboards. Look for local operators specializing in specific activities for personalized experiences and insider knowledge. Remember, safety first! Always check weather conditions, follow your guide's instructions, and respect the island's environment.

Water Sports and Activities

Forget the gym treadmill, trade it for Bora Bora's turquoise playground! Imagine yourself jet skiing like a tropical James Bond, leaving a trail of laughter and envy in your wake. Picture paddling a traditional outrigger canoe, feeling the rhythm of the waves carrying you to hidden coves where mermaids might actually be sunbathing (wink wink). Don't worry, landlubbers, there's adventure for you too! Lace up your hiking boots and conquer volcanic peaks, or chill on the beach with a cocktail, watching Polynesian gods (okay, maybe just buff surfers) shredding waves.

Get Your Adrenaline Pumping:

• **Jet Ski Like a Boss:** Feel the wind whip through your hair as you carve through the lagoon, volcanic peaks your backdrop. Bonus points for leaving dolphins in your dust (just kidding, don't actually do that). Rentals start around $100-$150 per hour – cheaper than therapy, way more fun!

• **Parasail Like a Bird (Without the Feathery Bits):** Soar high above the lagoon, the turquoise canvas stretching beneath you as you soak in panoramic views of Mount Otemanu and beyond. Think Instagram-worthy selfies with a side of bragging rights. Tours typically range from $80-$120 per person – a small price to pay for eternal glory (or at least until your next friend visits Bora Bora).

• **Shark & Ray Feeding:** Friend, Not Food: Embark on a thrilling encounter with nature's gentle giants. Observe blacktip reef sharks and majestic stingrays as they glide gracefully around you in their natural habitat. Remember, they're more interested in plankton than your toes (hopefully). Tours typically range from $150-$200 per person – not a bad price for facing your fears (or pretending you weren't scared at all).

Hiking Trails

Forget the beach bum life for a moment, adventure awaits on Bora Bora's land! Lace up your hiking boots and trade turquoise hues for verdant vistas on these epic trails:

Mount Otemanu: Summit Selfie for the Win
• **Challenge:** Conquer the island's iconic peak, a mighty 727 meters tall. Choose the guided hike for historical insights and cultural knowledge, or the 4x4 option for a breathtaking scenic drive.
• **Reward:** Panoramic views that will melt your Instagram followers' hearts. Witness the vast lagoon, neighboring islands, and the endless Pacific horizon – brag-worthy snaps guaranteed!
• **Pro Tip:** Pack water, good shoes, and your adventurous spirit. This moderate to challenging hike requires some effort, but the reward is worth the sweat (and maybe a post-hike cocktail).

Faanui Valley: Where History Whispers
• **Challenge:** Hike through lush valleys dotted with ancient Polynesian ruins, marae (temples), and remnants of stone fortresses. Imagine the whispers of forgotten warriors and the secrets buried beneath the earth.

- **Reward:** Immerse yourself in the island's rich history and cultural heritage. Learn about ancient rituals, societal structures, and the fascinating lives of Bora Bora's ancestors.
- **Pro Tip:** Combine this hike with a visit to the Faanui Cannons for stunning lagoon views and a dose of colonial history.

Matira Point: Hike, Swim, Relax, Repeat
- **Challenge:** This leisurely coastal trail winds along white sand beaches, volcanic rock formations, and swaying palm trees. Think picture-perfect scenery with minimal effort.
- **Reward:** Dip your toes in crystal-clear waters, snorkel amidst vibrant coral reefs, and soak up the island vibes. Unwind on pristine beaches and feel the sand between your toes.
- **Pro Tip:** Pack a picnic basket and make a day of it! This trail offers endless opportunities to relax, explore, and soak up the natural beauty of Bora Bora.

Valley of the Kings: Journey to the Past
- **Challenge:** Hike through a lush valley dotted with ancient marae, towering banyan trees, and remnants of royal settlements. This moderate trail offers cultural immersion and stunning natural beauty.

- **Reward:** Learn about the island's ancient royalty, their connection to the land, and the significance of these sacred sites. Imagine the lives of past kings and queens as you explore their former domain.
- **Pro Tip:** Combine this hike with a visit to the nearby Pearl Farm for a fascinating glimpse into Bora Bora's unique pearl industry.

Remember, land adventures in Bora Bora are not just about the physical challenge, but about connecting with the island's history, culture, and breathtaking scenery.

Biking Tours

Bora Bora isn't just a feast for the eyes; it's a playground for adrenaline seekers and leisurely explorers alike. What could be a more ideal way to encounter it all than by riding on two wheels? Trade the four-wheeled chariot for a trusty bicycle and embark on a biking adventure that will leave you breathless (from both the views and the exertion, depending on your chosen route!).

Embrace the Breeze:
- **Island Loop:** Circle the main island, feeling the wind in your hair and the sun on your back. Cruise

past charming villages, lush valleys, and iconic landmarks like Mount Otemanu. This moderate challenge (18 miles) takes about 6 hours, with plenty of stops for swimming, snacks, and photo ops. Rentals start around $20 per day.

• **Matira Beach Bliss:** Explore the island's most famous beach at your own pace. Cycle along the pristine coastline, stopping for dips in the turquoise waters and indulging in local delicacies at beachside cafes. This shorter, relaxed route (3-4 miles) is perfect for families and casual riders. Rentals are readily available near the beach.

• **Faanui Valley Immersion:** Delve deeper into the island's heart with a bike tour through the mystical Faanui Valley. Follow ancient paths, encounter historical sites, and soak in the lush greenery. This moderate terrain (6-8 miles) offers cultural insights and stunning natural beauty. Guided tours with knowledgeable local guides are highly recommended.

E-bike Adventures:
Don't let hills or fatigue dampen your island spirit! Opt for an e-bike and conquer challenging terrains with ease. Popular routes include the island loop and the Faanui Valley, allowing you to cover more

ground and enjoy breathtaking vistas without breaking a sweat. E-bike rentals cost slightly more than regular bikes but offer an effortless cycling experience.

Insider Tips:
• Wear comfortable clothing and sunscreen, and don't forget a hat and sunglasses.
• Carry water and snacks, especially on longer routes.
Respect local traffic laws and pedestrians.
• Consider guided tours for cultural insights and historical explanations.

Enjoy the journey, not just the destination! Take your time, savor the scenery, and feel the rhythm of the island.

Jeep Safaris

Forget the cushy confines of your air-conditioned resort jeep, trade it for an open-air adventure on a Bora Bora Jeep Safari! Buckle up for a bumpy, dusty, and undeniably thrilling journey that takes you off the beaten path and into the heart of the island's hidden gems. Here's why you should ditch the flip-flops and hop on board:

Unleash Your Inner Explorer

• **Off-Road Escapades:** Leave the paved roads behind and venture into the island's rugged interior. Navigate dusty trails, climb volcanic slopes, and conquer muddy puddles – adrenaline rush guaranteed!

• **Panoramic Vistas:** Witness Bora Bora from a whole new perspective. Reach lookout points inaccessible by car and gasp at the breathtaking panoramas of turquoise lagoons, lush valleys, and volcanic peaks stretching as far as the eye can see.

• **Hidden Gems Unveiled:** Discover secluded beaches hidden behind palm groves, ancient Polynesian marae (temples) tucked away in the wilderness, and charming villages untouched by mass tourism.

Dive into History and Culture

• **Time Travel to the Past:** Visit historical sites like WWII relics and remnants of ancient settlements. Learn about the island's fascinating past from knowledgeable guides and feel the connection to the land and its people.

• **Local Encounters:** Interact with friendly villagers, experience traditional practices like coconut weaving or pareo (sarong) making, and gain a deeper understanding of the local way of life.

- **Fruitful Delights:** Stop at roadside stalls and indulge in fresh, exotic fruits like pineapple, mango, and starfruit. Savor the local flavors and support the island's farmers.

Choose Your Adventure

- **Half-Day Thrill Ride:** Opt for a shorter expedition focusing on adrenaline-pumping off-road trails and breathtaking viewpoints. Perfect for adventurous spirits who want a taste of the wild side.
- **Full-Day Exploration:** Immerse yourself in a full-day adventure, combining historical sites, cultural encounters, and time for swimming and relaxation at secluded beaches. Ideal for those seeking a deeper connection to the island.
- **Sunset Safari:** Capture the magic of Bora Bora during the golden hour. Witness the sky ablaze with vibrant colors as you sip on local cocktails and enjoy breathtaking views. A romantic and unforgettable experience.

Embrace the bumpy ride, soak in the stunning scenery, and connect with the island's hidden gems and rich culture. It's an adventure you won't soon forget!

Exploring Local Markets

Bora Bora isn't just about picture-perfect beaches and luxurious resorts. It's also a treasure trove of vibrant culture and unique souvenirs waiting to be discovered at its bustling local markets. So, step away from the resort boutiques and immerse yourself in the authentic island experience:

A Sensory Feast:
• **Marae Maha Teavaroa:** This lively market bustles with activity every Tuesday and Friday morning. Explore stalls overflowing with fresh fruits and vegetables, locally caught seafood, fragrant spices, and handcrafted souvenirs. Witness the vibrant energy of locals bartering and sharing stories, creating a truly immersive experience.

• **Topiti Fautaua:** Held every Wednesday morning, this market near Vaitape village offers a delightful mix of local produce, sarongs, pareos, and handcrafted wood carvings. Don't miss the opportunity to sample delicious local snacks like poisson cru (raw fish marinated in coconut milk) and fruit smoothies.
• **Matira Village Market:** Nestled by Matira Beach, this charming market operates daily, offering a curated selection of souvenirs like pearl jewelry, shell necklaces, and locally made monoi oil.

Haggling is expected, making the shopping experience interactive and fun.

Beyond Souvenirs:

• **Art & Soul:** Discover the artistic spirit of Bora Bora at stalls showcasing woven baskets, intricate wood carvings, and colorful paintings depicting island life. Support local artisans and bring home a unique piece of art that captures the island's essence.

• **Pearl Power:** Bora Bora is renowned for its exquisite Tahitian pearls. Learn about the fascinating pearl farming process and browse stunning pearl jewelry at dedicated stalls or specialty shops within the markets.

• **A Taste of Paradise:** Take a culinary journey by purchasing locally produced jams, honey, vanilla beans, and spices. Recreate the island's flavors back home and share the delicious memories with loved ones.

Insider Tips:

• **Embrace the barter:** Haggling is part of the local market experience. Do your research beforehand and have fun negotiating for the best price.

- **Respectful photography:** Always ask permission before taking photos of locals, especially women and children.
- **Carry local currency:** Some vendors might not accept cards, so have Pacific francs on hand for convenient transactions.
- **Support sustainability:** Opt for eco-friendly souvenirs made from local materials and avoid purchasing items that exploit marine life or contribute to environmental damage.

Exploring local markets is more than just shopping; it's about connecting with the island's culture, supporting its communities, and creating lasting memories.

WELLNESS AND RELAXATION

Spa and Wellness Centers

Forget picture-perfect postcards – Bora Bora is an island, where turquoise lagoons serenade you, swaying palms whisper secrets, and every breath promises to melt away your stress. But beyond the visual and auditory feast lies a deeper treasure: a haven of dedicated sanctuaries designed to soothe your soul and rejuvenate your spirit. Get ready to embark on a journey through Bora Bora's spa and wellness scene, where each treatment is a tropical lullaby and every massage a one-way ticket to paradise. Buckle up, because we're about to dive into the island's wellness wonders, with approximate prices to help you plan your pampering escape.

Embrace the Island Rhythm (From $100 to $500 per treatment):

• **Nature's Open-Air Embrace:** Imagine open-air treatment pavilions (think $150-$200 per massage) where gentle breezes carry the scent of frangipani and the rhythmic lull of the ocean lulls you into a state of bliss. Picture volcanic black sand gently exfoliating your skin (around $100) followed by a dip in a natural freshwater pool nestled amidst lush greenery – all part of the Bora Bora spa experience. It's a synergy of nature's healing touch and expert pampering, and it doesn't get much more heavenly than that.

• **Indulge in Ancient Polynesian Traditions:** Unwind with ancient Tahitian massage techniques passed down through generations. Surrender to the rhythmic kneading of "Taurumi", a deep tissue massage designed to melt away tension (around $200), or experience the invigorating "Lomilomi", a holistic therapy that incorporates essential oils and chanting for a complete mind-body-spirit refresh (typically around $150-$200).

• **Go Local, Go Luxurious (Prices vary depending on spa and treatment):** Whether you seek the intimate charm of a boutique spa tucked away in a hidden cove or the opulent serenity of a resort's world-class wellness center, Bora Bora caters to every desire. Treat yourself to a signature ritual using locally sourced ingredients like coconut oil, volcanic sand, and exotic flowers (expect prices to range from $200-$500), each treatment infused with the island's unique spirit.

Unwind Your Way (Prices vary depending on spa and treatment):

• **Couples' Bliss:** Rekindle romance with a side-by-side massage on a private beach (think $300-$400 for a couple's massage), followed by a candlelit soak in a flower-strewn bath under a canopy of stars (prices vary depending on the spa's package). Some resorts even offer personalized couple's rituals inspired by Polynesian love legends, weaving intimacy into your wellness journey.

• **Solo Serenity:** Find your inner peace with a personalized yoga session overlooking the lagoon (around $50-$100), followed by a guided meditation in a sacred space (typically included in wellness retreats). Many spas offer solo wellness retreats designed to reconnect you with yourself in this breathtaking setting, with prices ranging from $500-$1,500 depending on the duration and inclusions.

• **Active Adventurers:** After conquering the island's hikes and watersports, soothe your muscles with a deep-tissue massage (around $200-$300) or indulge in a revitalizing body wrap using detoxifying marine extracts (typically $150-$200). Bora Bora's spas offer treatments specifically designed for active travelers, ensuring you're ready to explore more the next day.

Beyond the Massage:

• **Culinary Wellness (Prices vary depending on restaurant and menu):** Nourish your body from the inside out with locally sourced, organic cuisine crafted by chefs who understand the power of food to heal. Many spas offer healthy menus featuring fresh seafood, tropical fruits, and superfoods grown on the island. Expect to spend around $50-$100 per meal.

• **Cultural Immersion (Prices vary depending on activity):** Enhance your wellness journey by learning about the traditional healing practices of the Polynesian people. Participate in a kava ceremony, a social gathering known for its calming properties (around $50-$75), or attend a workshop on weaving natural remedies from local plants (prices vary depending on the workshop).

Remember:

• **Book in advance:** Popular spas, especially during peak season, tend to fill up quickly. Secure your appointments well ahead of your trip to avoid disappointment.

• **Consult a spa specialist:** Discuss your specific needs and preferences with the spa's team to ensure you choose the perfect treatment for your desired outcome.

- **Embrace the moment:** Disconnect from technology, silence your inner chatter, and allow yourself to be fully present in this haven of tranquility. Let Bora Bora's magic

Yoga and Meditation Retreats

Bora Bora isn't just about indulgent spa treatments – it's also a haven for soul-seekers yearning for deeper connection and inner peace. Enter the world of yoga and meditation retreats, where breathtaking landscapes become your practice mat and the rhythm of the ocean guides your breath. Immerse yourself in transformative experiences designed to awaken your senses, quiet your mind, and leave you feeling renewed.

Embrace the Elements (Prices vary depending on retreat & duration):
- **Beachfront Bliss:** Imagine practicing vinyasa flow as the sun rises over the lagoon, or meditating on a coral sand beach as waves gently lap the shore. Many retreats offer open-air studios perched on the water's edge, creating a natural sanctuary for your practice. Expect prices to range from $1,500-$3,000 per person for week-long retreats, including accommodation, meals, and yoga/meditation sessions.

• **Luxurious Tranquility:** If you prefer a touch of opulence, several resorts offer retreat packages within their stunning grounds. Think private bungalows with plunge pools, world-class spa facilities, and gourmet vegetarian cuisine alongside your daily yoga and meditation sessions. Prepare to splurge, with prices typically starting around $3,000-$5,000 per person for luxury retreats.

• **Eco-Conscious Immersion:** Connect with nature on a deeper level at eco-friendly retreats nestled amidst lush rainforests or on private islands. These retreats often incorporate sustainable practices, local ingredients, and cultural experiences into their programs, offering a truly holistic approach to wellness. Expect prices to fall between $1,000-$2,500 per person for eco-conscious retreats, depending on the level of amenities and exclusivity.

Find Your Practice (Styles & Levels):

• **Beginner-Friendly Retreats:** Don't let your experience level hold you back! Several retreats cater to newcomers, offering gentle Hatha yoga, guided meditations, and workshops on mindfulness and relaxation. These retreats are perfect for dipping your toes into the world of yoga and meditation, with prices typically starting around $1,000-$1,500 per person.

• **Intensive Exploration:** Are you an experienced yogi seeking to deepen your practice? Dive into advanced Ashtanga or Vinyasa sessions, explore restorative Yin yoga, or even try aerial yoga suspended above the lagoon. These retreats often attract like-minded practitioners and offer specialized workshops, with prices ranging from $2,000-$3,500 per person.

• **Mindfulness & Meditation Focus:** Retreats dedicated solely to meditation offer a powerful journey inward. Learn various meditation techniques, participate in silent mindfulness walks, and deepen your self-awareness in serene settings. Expect prices to be similar to beginner-friendly retreats, starting around $1,000-$1,500 per person.

Beyond the Asana

• **Cultural Connections:** Many retreats weave authentic Polynesian experiences into their programs, offering opportunities to learn traditional dance, connect with local healers, or participate in sacred ceremonies. Immersing yourself in the island's culture adds a unique dimension to your retreat experience.

• **Water Adventures:** Balance your inward journey with invigorating outdoor activities.

Kayaking through turquoise waters, snorkeling alongside vibrant coral reefs, or paddleboarding under the vast Polynesian sky - many retreats offer optional excursions to complement your practice.

Choosing Your Retreat:
• Consider your budget and desired level of luxury.
• Research the retreat's yoga style, teacher qualifications, and daily schedule.
• Explore the location, accommodation options, and any additional activities offered.
• Check out feedback from previous participants to gain an understanding of the overall experience.

Finding the perfect Bora Bora yoga and meditation retreat is about aligning your personal needs with the unique offerings of each program. So, close your eyes, imagine yourself practicing yoga on a pristine beach, and start planning your journey to inner peace in paradise!

Beachside Relaxation

Oh, imagine Bora Bora – it's not just a name, it's like Mother Nature decided to show off her A-game! We're talking crystal-clear lagoons giving your Instagram feed a run for its money, palm trees that probably have their own gossip club, and bungalows so dreamy, you'll feel like you've just stumbled into the VIP section of paradise. But wait, there's more! Beyond the picture-perfect scenes, Bora Bora is like that friend who surprises you with hidden talents. Need a spa day? Bora Bora got you covered. Craving some yoga zen? Pack your stretchy pants. Or maybe you just want to cozy up by the beach and let the waves do the talking – Bora Bora has got that too! Bora Bora: where even the palm trees are in on the secret to ultimate chill vibes.

Indulge in Tranquility at a Luxurious Spa:
• **Nature's Embrace:** Imagine open-air treatment pavilions perched above the lagoon, gentle breezes carrying the scent of frangipani, and the rhythmic lull of the ocean lulling you into a state of bliss. Indulge in a volcanic black sand exfoliation followed by a dip in a natural freshwater pool nestled amidst lush greenery – all part of the Bora Bora spa experience. Expect prices to range from $100 to $500 for individual treatments, depending on the spa and your chosen indulgence.

• **Ancient Polynesian Traditions:** Unwind with time-honored Tahitian massage techniques passed down through generations. Surrender to the rhythmic kneading of "Taurumi", a deep tissue massage designed to melt away tension (around

$200), or experience the invigorating "Lomilomi", a holistic therapy incorporating essential oils and chanting for complete mind-body-spirit refresh (typically around $150-$200).

• **Boutique Charm or Resort Opulence:** Whether you seek the intimate ambiance of a hidden gem spa or the world-class facilities of a resort sanctuary, Bora Bora caters to your desires. Treat yourself to a signature ritual using locally sourced ingredients like coconut oil, volcanic sand, and exotic flowers (prices typically range from $200-$500), each treatment infused with the island's unique spirit.

Find Harmony through Yoga & Meditation Retreats:

• **Beachfront Bliss:** Imagine practicing vinyasa flow as the sun rises over the lagoon, or meditating on a coral sand beach as waves gently lap the shore. Many retreats boast open-air studios on the water's edge, creating a breathtaking natural sanctuary for your practice. Expect week-long retreats with accommodation, meals, and yoga/meditation sessions to range from $1,500-$3,000 per person.

• **Luxurious Tranquility:** If indulgence is your middle name, several resorts offer retreat packages within their stunning grounds. Think private bungalows with plunge pools, world-class spa facilities, and gourmet vegetarian cuisine alongside your daily yoga and meditation sessions. Prepare to splurge, with prices typically starting around $3,000-$5,000 per person for luxury retreats.

• **Eco-Conscious Immersion:** Connect with nature on a deeper level at eco-friendly retreats nestled amidst lush rainforests or on private islands. These retreats often incorporate sustainable practices, local ingredients, and cultural experiences into their programs, offering a truly holistic approach to wellness. Expect prices to fall between $1,000-$2,500 per person for eco-conscious retreats, depending on the level of amenities and exclusivity.

Unwind Under the Sun on Pristine Beaches:

• **Claim Your Paradise:** Bora Bora boasts an array of beaches, each offering its own unique charm. Imagine sinking your toes into the powdery white sand of Matira Beach, where calm turquoise waters beckon you for a swim. For a touch of exclusivity, explore secluded beaches on private motus (islets). Remember, most resorts have private beach areas for their guests.

• **Embrace the Water:** Float weightlessly in the warm lagoon, snorkel amongst vibrant coral reefs teeming with colorful fish, or paddleboard across the glassy surface – feeling the gentle spray on your face. Whether you're an active adventurer or a sun-worshiper, the ocean in Bora Bora has something for everyone. Expect activities like snorkeling equipment rentals to start around $20-$30 per day, while paddleboard rentals range from $30-$50. Many resorts offer complimentary kayaks and paddleboards for their guests.

• **Indulge in Island-Style Pampering:** Rent a luxurious overwater bungalow, where your private deck becomes your personal relaxation haven. Imagine dipping into your plunge pool as the sun sets, indulging in an in-room massage with the sound of the waves as your soundtrack, or simply lying in a hammock, lulled by the gentle breeze. Overwater bungalows can range in price from $1,000 per night and upwards, depending on the specific resort and amenities.

Beyond the Relaxation:

• **Sunset Serenity:** Find a quiet spot on the beach as the sun dips below the horizon, painting the sky in fiery hues of orange, pink, and purple. Witness nature's breathtaking spectacle as the clouds catch the last rays, and listen to and listen to the gentle lapping of waves against the shore. Feel the cool sand beneath your feet and let the worries of the world melt away with the setting sun. Breathe in the fresh, salty air and savor the peacefulness of the moment.

Cultural Connections:
• Learn the art of weaving a coconut leaf hat: Experience the local culture by participating in a workshop where you learn this traditional skill passed down through generations.
• Immerse yourself in a ukulele serenade: Let the soothing melodies of traditional Polynesian music wash over you as you witness the sunset or enjoy a romantic dinner.
• Connect with friendly locals: Strike up a conversation with islanders and learn about their way of life, customs, and traditions. Get insider tips on hidden gems and authentic experiences.

Culinary Delights:
• **Savor fresh seafood dishes:** Indulge in local specialties like poisson cru (raw fish marinated in coconut milk and citrus), grilled mahi-mahi, and lobster cooked to perfection.
• **Tropical cocktails with a view:** Sip on exotic cocktails made with fresh fruits and local spirits while enjoying breathtaking vistas of the lagoon and mountains.

- **Dine under the stars:** Treat yourself to a romantic beachfront dinner where the twinkling night sky and gentle sound of waves create a magical ambiance.

Additional Information:
- This guide provides a starting point for your Bora Bora journey. Research specific resorts, activities, and cultural experiences to fit your interests and budget.
- Consider the time of year you plan to visit, as peak season (July-August) can be more crowded and expensive.

Be respectful of the local culture and environment. Leave only footprints and take only memories.

Remember, Bora Bora is an island that beckons you to slow down, connect with nature, and reconnect with yourself. Whether you choose to indulge in luxurious spa treatments, embark on a transformative yoga retreat, or simply relax on pristine beaches, allow the island's magic to work its wonders and leave you feeling truly rejuvenated.

SUSTAINABILITY AND RESPONSIBLE TOURISM

Eco-Friendly Practices

Bora Bora's beauty isn't just skin-deep. Beneath the turquoise waters and lush landscapes lies a rich cultural heritage and fragile ecosystem. As responsible travelers, it's our privilege to tread lightly and leave a positive footprint on this island paradise. Let's embrace eco-friendly practices that ensure Bora Bora's magic endures for generations to come.

• **Embrace the "Mana":** In Polynesian culture, "Mana" signifies spiritual energy and respect for the land. Channel this spirit by choosing eco-certified accommodations committed to renewable energy, water conservation, and waste reduction. Imagine waking up to the gentle lap of waves in your overwater bungalow, knowing your presence supports sustainable practices.

- **Dive into Conservation:** The vibrant coral reefs are Bora Bora's lifeblood. Opt for reef-safe sunscreen and diving operators dedicated to responsible practices. Witness the underwater wonders without harming the delicate ecosystem that sustains them. Every conscious choice protects vibrant fish, majestic manta rays, and breathtaking coral gardens.

- **Locally Sourced, Globally Conscious:** Savor the island's culinary scene with a sustainable twist. Seek restaurants that feature locally sourced ingredients, supporting family farms and reducing carbon footprint. Imagine indulging in fresh ahi tuna caught by local fishermen, knowing your meal empowers the community and respects the ocean's bounty.

- **Beyond the Bungalows:** Venture beyond the resort walls and connect with the island's culture. Choose local guides for hikes or bike tours, immersing yourself in the authentic spirit of Bora Bora. Support local artisans by purchasing hand-crafted souvenirs, each piece carrying a story and empowering the community's artistic heritage.

- **Reduce, Reuse, Replenish:** Pack wisely, minimizing single-use plastics and bringing refillable water bottles. Remember, even small actions like conserving water in your shower or opting for reusable shopping bags leave a positive impact. By embracing the "reduce, reuse, replenish" mantra, we collectively safeguard the island's precious resources.

• **Be an Ambassador, Not a Guest:** Share your eco-conscious enthusiasm with fellow travelers. Spread the message of responsible tourism, inspiring others to embrace sustainable practices. Together, we can ensure Bora Bora's magic remains enchanting for future generations.

Remember, your travel choices have the power to make a difference. By embracing eco-friendly practices, you become an active participant in preserving Bora Bora's natural beauty and cultural richness. So, let's embark on this captivating journey, leaving footprints of respect and ensuring paradise thrives for years to come.

Supporting Local Communities

Bora Bora isn't just a breathtaking destination; it's a vibrant community with a rich culture and distinct way of life. As responsible travelers, it's not just about minimizing our impact on the environment, but also about maximizing our positive influence on the people who call this island home. Let's explore ways to weave meaningful connections and support the local community during your visit:

- **Embrace Authentic Experiences:** Skip the generic tours and opt for locally-owned and operated excursions. Hike through lush rainforests led by knowledgeable guides who share their deep understanding of the island's natural wonders and cultural significance. Imagine paddling amidst the breathtaking scenery with a local fisherman, learning about traditional fishing techniques and the island's unique ecosystem.

- **Shop with Aloha:** Ditch the chain stores and embrace the vibrant local markets. Immerse yourself in the bustling atmosphere while supporting families and artisans by purchasing hand-crafted souvenirs. Every woven basket, intricate wood carving, or colorful pareo tells a story and empowers the community's artistic heritage. Remember, your purchases go directly to supporting local livelihoods and keeping cultural traditions alive.

- **Dine with a Purpose:** Indulge in the island's culinary scene at family-run restaurants and local cafes. Savor the authentic flavors prepared with fresh, locally sourced ingredients, knowing your meal directly benefits the community. Imagine enjoying a sunset dinner on the beach, where the warm hospitality and delicious food create an unforgettable experience that supports local businesses.

• **Spread the Aloha Spirit:** Learn a few basic Tahitian phrases like "Mauruuru roa" (thank you) and "Iaorana" (hello). Engaging with locals in their language shows respect and opens doors to genuine connections. You might even be invited to participate in a cultural event or learn a traditional dance, creating memories that go beyond the typical tourist experience.

• **Give Back with Purpose:** Many organizations work tirelessly to preserve Bora Bora's environment and cultural heritage. Consider volunteering your time at a local conservation project, helping clean beaches, or contributing to community development initiatives. Even a few hours of your time can make a significant impact, leaving a lasting positive mark on the island.

• **Be a Respectful Guest:** Remember, you're visiting someone's home. Dress modestly when visiting cultural sites and respect local customs and traditions. Ask permission before taking photos of people, and dispose of your trash responsibly. By demonstrating cultural sensitivity and responsible behavior, you contribute to a positive image of tourists and leave a respectful impression.

By making conscious choices to support local communities, you enrich your own travel experience and create a ripple effect of positive change. Remember, every dollar spent locally, every conversation shared, and every act of kindness contributes to a more sustainable and equitable future for Bora Bora.

Leave No Trace: Responsible Travel Tips

Bora Bora's breathtaking beauty comes
with a delicate balance – a responsibility to tread lightly and ensure its magic endures for generations. Embracing the "Leave No Trace" principles ensures your adventures leave only positive footprints:

• **Tread Softly:** Stick to designated trails and avoid trampling on fragile vegetation. Remember, even seemingly harmless footsteps can disrupt delicate ecosystems. Imagine exploring ancient marae (temples) with respect, appreciating their cultural significance without disturbing the surrounding areas.
• **Waste Not, Want Not:** Pack reusable bags, water bottles, and food containers. Avoid single-use plastics and dispose of all waste responsibly in

designated bins. Imagine enjoying a picnic on the beach without leaving behind any trace, keeping the paradise pristine for future visitors.

• **Respect the Reef:** Opt for reef-safe sunscreen and avoid touching or standing on fragile coral. Choose boat operators committed to sustainable practices and responsible anchoring. Imagine snorkeling amidst vibrant coral gardens, teeming with life, knowing your presence respects this underwater wonderland.

• **Leave What You Find:** Don't remove natural treasures like rocks, shells, or coral – they belong to the island's ecosystem. Instead, capture memories through photographs and leave the beauty intact for others to enjoy. Imagine leaving the beach as you found it, pristine and untouched, ensuring others can experience its magic too.

• **Minimize Campfire Impact:** If campfires are permitted, use designated fire rings and collect deadwood only. Extinguish fires completely with water and ensure ashes are cool before leaving. Imagine gazing at the starlit sky by a crackling fire, leaving no trace upon your departure.

• **Be Wildlife Wise:** Observe wildlife from a safe distance and avoid disturbing their natural behavior. Don't feed animals, as human food can harm them. Imagine witnessing majestic manta rays gliding gracefully by, respecting their space and preserving the natural wonder of their presence.

• **Be Considerate of Others:** Respect the peace and tranquility of the island. Keep noise levels down, especially in sacred areas and near local communities. Imagine sharing the serenity of a sunrise meditation on the beach, mindful of not disturbing others seeking the same tranquility.

Remember, every responsible action adds up. By embracing these "Leave No Trace" principles, you become a steward of Bora Bora's paradise, ensuring its magic thrives for generations to come.

Hidden Gems and Off-the-Beaten-Path Adventures

So, you've already marveled at Mount Otemanu's majesty, snorkeled with technicolor fish, and perfected your "island time" nap in your overwater bungalow. What's next for the Bora Bora veteran like yourself? Fear not, intrepid explorer, for paradise still holds secrets waiting to be unraveled! We're talking hidden gems that'll make you chuckle and say, "Why didn't I do this sooner?"

1. Ditch the Lagoon Cruise, Kayak to Paradise: Trade the crowded catamaran for a kayak adventure. Paddle towards secluded motus (islets) fringed by impossibly white sand and guarded by swaying palm trees. Imagine basking on your own private beach, feeling like Robinson Crusoe (minus the unfortunate coconut incident). Bonus points for befriending a hermit crab named Wilson (not guaranteed).

2. Hike Like Indiana Jones (Without the Snakes): Ditch the resort gym and embark on a trek through the lush Faanui Valley. Climb ancient volcanic peaks, discover hidden waterfalls cascading into emerald pools, and unearth remnants of Polynesian settlements. Just remember, the only snakes you'll encounter are probably friendly geckos searching for kisses (don't judge, they're cute).

3. Learn to Surf Where Legends Ride: Ditch the jet ski (been there, done that, splashed the resort staff), and try your hand at surfing at Pointe Matira. Catch waves alongside local champions, soak in epic sunsets, and wipe out spectacularly (it's part of the learning curve, embrace it!). Imagine the bragging rights you'll have back home: "Yeah, I surfed in Bora Bora, no big deal." (Insert nonchalant shrug here.)

4. Go Deep with a Local Dive Master: Ditch the crowded reef dives and embark on an underwater adventure with a local guide. Explore hidden dive sites teeming with unique marine life, from playful dolphins to elusive reef sharks (don't worry, they're more interested in fish than fancy sunglasses). Imagine emerging from the depths, feeling like Jacques Cousteau, minus the red beanie (it might clash with your swimsuit).

5. Get Cultured with a Cooking Class (and Laughter): Ditch the resort buffets and learn the secrets of Polynesian cuisine in a fun and interactive cooking class. Imagine giggling your way through attempts to grate coconut with a dull grater, learning traditional recipes passed down for generations, and finally devouring your culinary masterpiece (even if it looks a bit like abstract art).

Remember, Bora Bora's magic extends far beyond the resort walls. So, ditch the routine, embrace the unexpected, and discover the island's hidden gems with a dash of humor and a sprinkle of adventure. You might just surprise yourself (and maybe even make some new furry friends with excellent taste in coconuts).

Special Events and Festivals

Alright, fellow Bora Bora aficionados! Craving something more than lounging in your luxurious overwater bungalow (don't get me wrong, it's amazing)? Look no further! Let's ditch the predictable and dive headfirst into the island's electrifying special events and festivals, where culture explodes, locals unwind, and your Instagram feed will thank you.

1. Heiva i Bora Bora (July): Brace yourself for a Polynesian extravaganza! Imagine pulsating drumbeats, mesmerizing dancers adorned in vibrant costumes, and fire knife performances that'll leave you speechless (and maybe a little singed if you stand too close, but hey, that's part of the thrill!). Witness traditional competitions like coconut weaving and stone-lifting (don't even think about trying that at home, unless you want your vacation to turn into a medical emergency). It's a sensory overload in the best way possible, leaving you with memories that'll make your friends back home green with envy.

2. Hawaiki Nui Va'a (November): Calling all adrenaline junkies and avid spectators! Witness the epic arrival of the Hawaiki Nui Va'a, a three-day outrigger canoe race traversing 80 miles of open ocean. Imagine hundreds of brightly painted canoes charging towards the shores of Matira Beach, cheered on by a vibrant crowd. It's a display of athletic prowess, cultural pride, and pure excitement that'll leave you hoarse from cheering (and maybe a little sunburnt, so don't forget the sunscreen!).

3. Tahiti Pearl Regatta (May/June): Calling all sailing enthusiasts and wannabe pirates (minus the plundering, of course)! Watch majestic yachts from around the world battle it out in a thrilling race between the islands of Tahiti. Imagine sipping tropical cocktails on the beach while cheering on your favorite vessel, feeling like you're part of a real-life Pirates of the Caribbean movie (minus the questionable hygiene and scurvy). It's a chance to witness nautical mastery and indulge in island vibes, all in one go.

4. FIFO - Pacific International Documentary Film Festival (February): Calling all cinephiles and documentary enthusiasts! Dive into the captivating world of storytelling at the FIFO festival. Imagine screening thought-provoking documentaries under the starry Polynesian sky, followed by lively discussions and cultural performances. It's a chance to broaden your horizons, engage with global issues, and maybe even discover your inner film critic (who secretly loves popcorn, we all do).

5. Village de Noël (December): Calling all festive spirits and those who like their Christmas with a tropical twist! Witness the transformation of Vaitape into a charming Christmas village, complete with twinkling lights, festive decorations, and local artisans selling unique gifts. Imagine indulging in delicious Polynesian Christmas treats, swaying to lively carols with a ukulele twist, and maybe even spotting Santa arriving on a outrigger canoe (because why not?). It's a unique blend of island flair and holiday cheer that'll leave you feeling warm and fuzzy inside (and maybe a little sugared up from all the treats).

Remember, Bora Bora's magic isn't just about picture-perfect beaches and luxurious resorts. It's about immersing yourself in the island's vibrant culture, celebrating its traditions, and creating memories that go beyond the ordinary. So, ditch the predictable, embrace the festive spirit, and discover the soul of Bora Bora through its unforgettable events and festivals. Just don't forget your dancing shoes, camera, and maybe a sarong if you want to join the fun (cultural appropriation always requires respect, of course). Happy exploring!

Tips for Returning Travelers

Ah, the familiar embrace of Bora Bora's turquoise waters and Mount Otemanu's majestic peak. Welcome back, seasoned traveler! You've conquered the overwater bungalows, mastered the art of "island time," and likely have a collection of envy-inducing photos. But fear not, paradise still holds surprises for the returning adventurer. Here are some tips to spice up your second (or tenth) Bora Bora escapade:

1. Go Local, Skip the Tourist Traps: Ditch the crowded excursions and opt for authentic experiences. Befriend a local guide who can show you hidden waterfalls, secret beaches, and family-run restaurants serving up mouthwatering dishes passed down for generations. Remember, sometimes the best souvenirs are memories, not trinkets.

2. Embrace the Slow Lane: You've already ticked off the "must-see" sights. Now, relax and immerse yourself in the laid-back island pace. Rent a scooter and explore the winding coastal roads, stopping at roadside stands for fresh fruit and friendly chats with locals. Remember, slowing down allows you to truly savor the island's essence.

3. Hone Your Adventurous Spirit: Unleash your inner Robinson Crusoe! Kayak to secluded motus, hike untouched mountain trails, or try stand-up paddleboarding across the lagoon. Remember, stepping outside your comfort zone often leads to the most rewarding experiences. (Just don't forget the sunscreen and a healthy dose of caution!)

4. Give Back & Leave a Positive Mark: This time, go beyond enjoying the beauty. Volunteer at a local conservation project, donate to a community initiative, or simply support local businesses by buying souvenirs directly from artisans. Remember, responsible tourism enriches not only your journey but also the lives of those who call Bora Bora home.

5. Deepen Your Cultural Connection: Take a Tahitian language class, learn the art of weaving coconut leaves, or participate in a traditional dance workshop. Remember, cultural immersion allows you to appreciate the soul of the island beyond the postcard-perfect scenery.

6. Relive Your Favorite Moments: Return to the restaurant where you shared a romantic dinner, revisit the secluded beach where you watched the sunset, or hike the trail that took your breath away the first time. Remember, revisiting cherished memories adds a layer of nostalgia and appreciation to your experience.

7. Connect with Fellow Travelers: Share your love for Bora Bora with others! Strike up conversations with fellow travelers, swap stories, and recommend hidden gems you've discovered. Remember, connecting with others enriches your journey and creates a sense of shared adventure.

8. Pack Light, Pack Smart: This time, ditch the unnecessary souvenirs and focus on packing experiences. Remember, less stuff means more space for memories (and maybe that extra cocktail at sunset).

9. Embrace the Unexpected: Be open to spontaneity! Let the island guide you. A chance encounter with a local, a sudden change in plans, or an unexpected downpour might lead to your most memorable moment. Remember, sometimes the best adventures are the ones you don't plan for.

10. Savor the Moment: This might be your second (or tenth) trip, but the magic of Bora Bora never fades. Breathe in the fresh air, feel the sand between your toes, and truly appreciate the moment. Remember, paradise isn't just a place; it's a state of mind.

So, welcome back, intrepid traveler! May your second (or tenth) Bora Bora adventure be filled with laughter, discoveries, and memories that last a lifetime. Just remember, the true magic lies not just in the sights, but in the way you experience them. Now, go forth and explore, seasoned wanderer! Bora Bora awaits your return with open arms (and maybe a refreshing Mai Tai).

PRACTICAL TIPS AND SAFETY

Health and Safety Guidelines

As you gear up for your exciting return to Bora Bora, let's prioritize both the thrill of adventure and the comfort of knowing you're well-prepared for a safe and healthy trip. Here's a handy guide to essential health and safety guidelines:

Before You Go:
- **Vaccinations:** Consult your doctor to ensure you're up-to-date on recommended vaccinations, including Hepatitis A & B, Tetanus, and Typhoid. Depending on your activities, consider Rabies and Dengue Fever protection.
- **Travel Insurance:** Unexpected situations can arise, so secure comprehensive travel insurance covering medical emergencies, trip cancellations, and lost luggage.
- **Medications:** Pack enough of your personal medications and essential over-the-counter remedies like pain relievers, antihistamines, and antidiarrheals. Keep prescriptions in their original containers.

Island Essentials:

• **Sun Protection:** Pack reef-safe sunscreen with SPF 30+ and protective clothing like hats and sunglasses to shield yourself from the tropical sun.
Insect Repellent: Mosquitoes and other insects might pose a nuisance. Use a DEET-containing insect repellent recommended by health experts.

• **Drinking Water:** While tap water in major resorts and Tahiti is generally safe, bottled water is readily available and recommended for excursions.

• Footwear: Opt for sturdy sandals or water shoes for exploring rocky terrain and navigating the lagoon's wonders.

Safety Tips:

• **Ocean Respect:** Be mindful of currents, weather conditions, and your swimming abilities. Stick to designated swimming areas and use life jackets when necessary.

• **Reef Reverence:** Avoid touching or standing on coral reefs, as it damages this delicate ecosystem. Choose reef-safe sunscreen and boat operators with responsible practices.

• **Cultural Awareness:** Dress modestly when visiting sacred sites and respect local customs and traditions. Ensure to ask for permission before photographing individuals.

- **Staying Secure:** Keep valuables in a safe place like your hotel safe or use a money belt when carrying cash. Stay vigilant about your surroundings, especially in crowded places.
- **Emergency Numbers:** Save the emergency contact numbers for the local police, ambulance, and medical services on your phone for quick access.

Remember, being informed and prepared allows you to fully embrace the magic of Bora Bora without unnecessary worries. So, pack your sense of adventure, follow these essential tips, and create unforgettable memories that will last a lifetime!

Communication and Language

While basking in Bora Bora's beauty, navigating communication can add another layer of adventure. Here are some tips to ensure smooth sailing:

- **Embrace the Bilingual Advantage:** French is the official language, but Tahitian (Reo Maohi) is widely spoken. Learning a few basic phrases in both languages goes a long way. Start with "Iaorana" (hello) and "Mauruuru roa" (thank you) in Tahitian and "Bonjour" (hello) and "Merci beaucoup" (thank you) in French.

• **Gestures Speak Volumes:** A smile, a nod, or a thumbs-up can often bridge language gaps. Don't be afraid to use hand gestures and facial expressions to convey your meaning.

• **Pocket Phrasebooks and Apps:** Invest in a bilingual phrasebook or download a translation app for quick reference. Remember, pronunciation is key, so practice basic phrases before your trip.

• **Embrace Patience and Humor:** Communication hiccups are inevitable. Be patient, laugh at misunderstandings, and enjoy the process of learning a new language and culture.

• **Feel free to request assistance from the locals whenever needed.** Many islanders are multilingual and happy to assist, especially if you attempt a greeting in their language.

• **Utilize Resort Resources:** Most resorts have staff members who speak English and other languages. They can help with translations, recommendations, and navigating local customs.

• **Technology to the Rescue:** Translation apps and devices can be helpful, but remember they might not always be accurate. Use them as a starting point, not a complete solution.

- **Embrace Non-Verbal Communication:** Learn essential Tahitian numbers (useful for bargaining), and point if needed. Use pictures or drawings to illustrate your requests.
- **Respect Goes a Long Way:** Remember, you're a guest in their country. Be respectful of the local language and culture, and your efforts will be appreciated.

By embracing these tips and a spirit of open-mindedness, you'll navigate the language landscape of Bora Bora with confidence and create meaningful connections with its people. After all, communication is often about the heart, not just the words.

Currency and Banking

When venturing into paradise, understanding the financial landscape ensures a smooth and worry-free experience. Here's your guide to navigating Bora Bora's currency and banking system:

Local Currency:
- The official currency in Bora Bora, and all of French Polynesia, is the CFP Franc (XPF). It's important to note that this is distinct from the Swiss Franc (CHF).

Euros are widely accepted in tourist areas, but the exchange rate might not be as favorable as using XPF.

US dollars are accepted in some places, but again, not always at the best rates.

• **Exchanging Currency:**

You can exchange your currency at the airport upon arrival, but rates might be higher. Consider exchanging smaller amounts to tide you over initially.

Most hotels and resorts offer currency exchange services, but compare rates before going with their convenience.

Banks and authorized exchange offices will typically offer the best exchange rates. Look for "Bureau de Change" signs.

• **Payment Methods:**

Credit cards (Visa and Mastercard) are widely accepted in major resorts, restaurants, and stores. Check for acceptance fees before swiping.

ATMs are readily available in major towns and resorts. Notify your bank about your travel arrangements to prevent card blocking.

• While tipping is not mandatory, it's appreciated for good service. A small percentage of the bill or a few XPF coins are customary.

Additional Tips:
• Consider traveler's checks for backup, although their use is declining.
• Carry some small denomination XPF for taxis, local markets, and tipping.
• Be mindful of ATM withdrawal fees and daily limits.
• Keep receipts for currency exchange and transactions for record-keeping and potential refunds.

By understanding these tips and familiarizing yourself with the local currency, you can navigate Bora Bora's financial waters with ease.

Local Etiquette

Beyond breathtaking landscapes and turquoise waters, Bora Bora boasts a rich cultural tapestry. To truly immerse yourself in its magic, respecting local customs and etiquette is key. Here's your guide to navigating the island's social landscape with grace and understanding:
• **Dress Modestly:** When visiting sacred sites like marae (temples) or attending cultural events, opt for covered clothing that respects local sensibilities. Avoid overly revealing swimwear or beachwear in these settings.

• **Greetings and Farewells:** A friendly smile and a "Iaorana" (hello) in Tahitian will go a long way. When shaking hands, use a gentle and respectful grip. A slight nod or bow is also an appropriate greeting. To say goodbye, use "Mauruuru roa" (thank you) followed by "Nana" (goodbye).

• **Gift-Giving Etiquette:** If you wish to offer a gift, opt for local handicrafts, flowers, or food items. Remember, it's the thought that counts. Always present gifts with both hands and avoid giving sharp objects, which can be symbolic of bad luck.

• **As earlier stated regarding tipping, while it's not obligatory, it is welcomed for excellent service.** A small percentage of the bill (around 10-15%) or a few XPF coins are customary. Remember, a genuine "Mauruuru roa" with a smile can convey your appreciation as well.

• **Public Displays of Affection:** Public displays of affection are generally reserved for private settings. Opt for respectful hand-holding or a light embrace over passionate displays.

• **Photography:** Always ask permission before taking photos of people, especially during cultural events or religious ceremonies. Respect their privacy and avoid using flash photography in sensitive situations.

• **Be Mindful of Sacred Sites:** Treat marae and other sacred sites with reverence. Dress modestly, avoid loud noises, and refrain from touching or climbing on structures.

• **Bargaining with Respect:** While bargaining is customary in local markets, do so politely and respectfully. Avoid being overly aggressive, and remember, the aim is to enjoy the interaction and appreciate the craftsmanship, not just secure the lowest price.

• **Embrace the Flow:** Island life moves at a slower pace. Be patient, avoid rushing locals, and appreciate the relaxed, laid-back attitude. Embrace the "island time" and savor the present moment.

Remember, cultural etiquette is about showing respect and understanding for the local way of life. By following these simple guidelines, you'll not only avoid faux pas but also foster genuine connections and create a positive impact on your Bora Bora journey. So, embrace the spirit of "aroha" (love) and respect, and let the island's warmth and beauty enchant you!

ITINERARY

7-Day Adventure Escapade

This itinerary is a starting point, designed to be customized based on your interests, preferences, and desired activity level. Remember, Bora Bora is all about soaking up the island vibes and creating unique memories. Feel free to mix and match suggestions or add your own discoveries!

Day 1:
• **Morning:** Arrive in Bora Bora, settle into your overwater bungalow, and soak in the breathtaking views. Enjoy a leisurely breakfast with stunning lagoon panoramas.
• **Afternoon:** Take a guided jet ski tour around the island, exploring hidden coves, visiting a motu (islet), and snorkeling in crystal-clear waters. Relax on a pristine beach, soaking up the sun and the serenity.
• **Evening:** Savor a romantic sunset dinner cruise, indulging in delicious Polynesian cuisine while watching the sky transform into a kaleidoscope of colors.

Day 2:
• **Morning:** Embark on a cultural adventure with a local guide. Learn about Polynesian traditions, visit a marae (temple), and witness a demonstration of traditional crafts like pareo making or coconut weaving.
• **Afternoon:** Go on a kayak tour through the lagoon, discovering secluded beaches and encountering playful manta rays or colorful fish. Enjoy a relaxing picnic lunch on a secluded motu.
• **Evening:** Attend a lively Polynesian dance performance, immersing yourself in the vibrant music, storytelling, and mesmerizing fire knife dance.

Day 3:
• **Morning:** Hike to the summit of Mount Otemanu (weather permitting) for breathtaking panoramic views of the island and the lagoon. Alternatively, choose a shorter hike with scenic viewpoints.
• **Afternoon:** Enjoy a relaxing afternoon at a luxurious spa, indulging in pampering treatments with locally sourced ingredients like coconut oil and monoi.
• **Evening:** Experience a traditional "poisson cru" (raw fish salad) dinner prepared by a local family,

followed by stargazing on the beach under the Milky Way.

Day 4:
• **Morning:** Learn to stand-up paddleboard (SUP) in the calm lagoon, enjoying a unique perspective of the underwater world and the surrounding beauty.
• **Afternoon:** Take a diving or snorkeling excursion to explore the vibrant coral reefs teeming with colorful fish, turtles, and other marine life. Witness the majestic underwater world firsthand.
• **Evening:** Enjoy a delicious "ahimaa" (Tahitian feast) at a local restaurant, showcasing a variety of traditional dishes cooked in an underground oven.

Day 5:
• **Morning:** Rent a scooter and explore the island's winding roads, stopping at local villages, pearl farms, and souvenir shops. Enjoy fresh coconuts and tropical fruits from roadside stalls.
• **Afternoon:** Visit the Lagoonarium, an underwater viewing area where you can observe various marine life without getting wet. Learn about the island's ecosystem and conservation efforts.
• **Evening:** Participate in a traditional Polynesian cooking class, learning the secrets of preparing local favorites like poisson cru and ma'a tahiti (chicken

with taro leaves). Enjoy your culinary creations for dinner.

Day 6:
• **Morning:** Relax and rejuvenate with a yoga session on the beach, surrounded by the calming sounds of the waves and the tropical breeze.
• **Afternoon:** Take a boat trip to a private motu for a secluded beach experience. Enjoy swimming, sunbathing, and a picnic lunch in your own personal paradise.
• **Evening:** Watch the sunset from your overwater bungalow, indulging in cocktails and reflecting on the memories you've created.

Day 7:
• **Morning:** Enjoy a leisurely breakfast, pack your bags, and depart from Bora Bora with a heart full of memories and a renewed sense of island bliss.

Additional Activities:
• Visit the Pearl Farm & Museum to learn about the fascinating process of pearl cultivation and admire exquisite Tahitian black pearls.
• Take a boat trip to a nearby island like Raiatea or Taha'a for a day of exploration and cultural immersion.

- Participate in a watersports activity like parasailing, waterskiing, or wakeboarding for an adrenaline rush.
- Attend a local church service to experience the island's vibrant spiritual culture and witness traditional attire and music.

Remember, this is just a suggestion. Feel free to adjust the itinerary based on your interests, fitness level, and budget. The most important thing is to relax, embrace the island spirit, and create memories that will last a lifetime!

10-Day Cultural Exploration

This 10-day itinerary delves deeper into the heart and soul of Bora Bora, offering a richer cultural experience beyond breathtaking landscapes and luxurious resorts. Immerse yourself in local traditions, connect with the community, and discover hidden gems, creating memories that transcend the typical tourist experience.

Day 1-3:
• **Cultural Immersion:** Begin with a guided tour of Vaitape, the main village, visiting the local market, artisan shops, and the Territorial Museum of Archaeology and Ethnology. Immerse yourself in

the vibrant colors, local crafts, and rich history of the island.

• **Homestay Experience:** Opt for a homestay in a local village for a few nights. Live alongside a family, learn about their daily lives, participate in traditional activities like weaving or fishing, and enjoy authentic home-cooked meals.

• **Polynesian Dance Workshop:** Join a Polynesian dance workshop and learn the graceful movements, powerful storytelling, and captivating rhythms that tell the island's stories. Be prepared to move your body, connect with the cultural spirit, and maybe even perform alongside locals.

Day 4-6:

• **Island Hike & Legends:** Embark on a moderate hike to Faanui Valley, discovering ancient marae (temples), hidden waterfalls, and lush vegetation. Listen to local legends from your guide, gaining deeper insight into the island's spiritual connection and cultural significance.

• **Cooking Class & Feast:** Participate in a hands-on cooking class, learning the secrets of preparing traditional Polynesian dishes like poisson cru, ma'a tahiti, and poe (fruit pudding). Enjoy your culinary creations alongside the instructor and other participants, fostering cultural exchange and delicious memories.

• **Traditional Healing Workshop:** Experience a traditional healing session with a local "taua" (healer), using natural remedies and ancient techniques to learn about their holistic approach to well-being and connect with the island's deep understanding of nature.

Day 7-9:
• **Island Hopping Adventure:** Venture beyond Bora Bora and explore neighboring islands like Raiatea, the cradle of Polynesian culture, or Taha'a, known for its vanilla plantations and pearl farms. Witness diverse landscapes, unique traditions, and the warmth of island hospitality on each island.
• **Attend a Local Festival:** If your dates coincide, immerse yourself in the vibrant energy of a local festival. Experience traditional music, dance performances, food stalls, and handicraft demonstrations, celebrating the island's culture and connecting with the community spirit.
• **Volunteer Opportunity:** Give back to the island by volunteering at a local conservation project, helping with beach cleanups, or assisting at a community center. Make a positive impact and gain deeper understanding of local challenges and initiatives.

Day 10:
• **Farewell Ritual:** Before departing, participate in a traditional "farewell" ceremony with your homestay family or tour guide. Exchange gifts, share stories, and express your gratitude for the unique cultural experience you received.

Additional Activities:
• Learn basic Tahitian phrases and practice with locals to connect on a deeper level.
• Attend a Sunday church service to witness the island's strong faith and vibrant music.
• Take a boat tour to a pearl farm and learn about the sustainable cultivation process and the cultural significance of pearls.
• Enjoy a relaxing evening with live music at a local bar, soaking up the island's laid-back atmosphere and connecting with fellow travelers.

Lovers' Retreat

This 7-day itinerary is specially crafted for couples seeking a luxurious escape filled with shared experiences, romantic moments, and unforgettable memories.

Day 1:

• **Arrival in Paradise:** Arrive in style with a private helicopter transfer directly to your luxurious overwater bungalow. Savor breathtaking views of the turquoise lagoon and toast to your romantic adventure with champagne on your private deck.

• **Sunset Sail & Snorkel:** Embark on a private sunset sail, enjoying gentle breezes, stunning scenery, and delicious canapés as the sun paints the sky with vibrant hues. Snorkel hand-in-hand amidst vibrant coral reefs teeming with colorful fish, creating a magical underwater experience.

• **Candlelit Dinner on the Beach:** Indulge in a gourmet dinner prepared by a private chef on a secluded beach. Under the twinkling stars and the gentle sound of waves, savor delicious dishes, personalized service, and intimate conversation.

Day 2:

• **Couples Spa Treatment:** Enjoy a pampering couples spa treatment, choosing from traditional Polynesian massages, aromatherapy rituals, or rejuvenating facials. Relax in the serene ambiance, reconnect with each other, and emerge feeling refreshed and loved-up.

• **Private Island Getaway:** Rent a private motu (islet) for the day. Enjoy complete seclusion, swim in crystal-clear waters, sunbathe on pristine sand,

and have a picnic lunch prepared with your preferences. Disconnect from the world and revel in each other's company.

• **Stargazing on the Lagoon:** Rent a paddleboard or kayak and drift into the calm lagoon after sunset. Lie back and marvel at the breathtaking Milky Way galaxy above, sharing heartfelt conversations and romantic moments under the vast starlit sky.

Day 3:

• **Couples' Cooking Class:** Participate in a fun and interactive couples' cooking class, learning the secrets of preparing Tahitian delicacies like poisson cru and ma'a tahiti. Laugh together, unleash your culinary creativity, and enjoy a delicious feast of your creations.

• **Private Jet Ski Tour:** Explore the island's hidden coves and secluded beaches on a thrilling private jet ski tour. Hold on tight, splash around, and enjoy breathtaking views together, creating an exhilarating and unforgettable adventure.

• **Romantic Dinner Cruise:** Sail into the sunset on a private dinner cruise, indulging in gourmet cuisine, attentive service, and breathtaking panoramas. Toast to your love, share heartfelt moments, and capture memories that will last a lifetime.

Day 4:

• **Sunrise Hike to Mount Otemanu:** Hike hand-in-hand to the summit of Mount Otemanu (weather permitting) for breathtaking panoramic views of the island and the lagoon at sunrise. Witness the magical colors as the day awakens, sharing a romantic and unforgettable moment.

• **Pearl Farm & Jewelry Boutique:** Discover the fascinating world of pearl cultivation at a local pearl farm. Choose a unique pearl jewelry piece as a symbol of your love, a timeless reminder of your Bora Bora adventure.

• **Relaxing Sunset & Cocktails:** Unwind on your private deck as the sun sets, sipping tropical cocktails and reminiscing about your shared experiences. Savor the tranquility of the moment and the beauty of being together in paradise.

Day 5:

• **Underwater Exploration:** Dive or snorkel hand-in-hand amidst the vibrant coral reefs, discovering a mesmerizing underwater world. Witness playful dolphins, colorful fish, and majestic manta rays, creating a shared adventure filled with wonder and awe.

• **Romantic Polynesian Dance Show:** Immerse yourselves in the vibrant music and captivating storytelling of a Polynesian dance show. Be mesmerized by the graceful movements and powerful energy, celebrating the island's culture and sharing a unique experience.

Day 6:

• **Couple's Massage on the Beach:** Relax and reconnect with a couples' massage on the beach, listening to the gentle waves and feeling the warm sand beneath you. Unwind, rejuvenate, and deepen your connection in this serene setting.

• **Farewell Dinner at a Local Restaurant:** Savor a delicious farewell dinner at a local restaurant, enjoying authentic Polynesian cuisine and the warm hospitality of the island. Share stories, laughter, and gratitude for your magical escape before departing from paradise.

Day 7:

• **Departure with Lasting Memories:** Depart from Bora Bora with hearts full of love, memories etched in your soul, and a renewed appreciation for your bond. Carry the magic of Bora Bora and the spirit of your romantic retreat wherever you go.

Remember: This is a starting point, personalize it! Add activities that reflect your shared interests, adjust the pace, and embrace the spirit of spontaneity. Bora Bora is your canvas, paint your perfect romantic escape!

CONCLUSION

Fond Farewell to Bora Bora

As your Bora Bora adventure draws to a close, bittersweet emotions may stir. The turquoise waters, the rhythmic sway of palm trees, the warmth of the sun-kissed sand – these memories will forever be woven into the fabric of your soul. But don't let goodbye dampen the joy of what you've experienced. Instead, embrace the farewell with a heart brimming with gratitude and a spirit infused with the island's magic.

Whispers of Paradise:

• **Recall the Sunrise Spectacle:** Close your eyes and remember the first sunrise you witnessed in Bora Bora. The gentle awakening of the lagoon, the fiery hues painting the sky, the soft chirping of birds – a natural beauty etched in your memory.

• **Feel the Rhythm of the Ocean:** Relive the gentle rocking of your overwater bungalow, the rhythmic lull of the waves, the cool caress of the ocean breeze. Let the island's pulse resonate within you, a calming melody you can revisit anytime.

• **Treasure the Dance of Colors:** From the vibrant greens of Mount Otemanu to the turquoise depths of the lagoon, the coral reefs bursting with life to the fiery sunsets that painted the sky – hold onto these colorful snapshots, a visual feast for your soul.

• **Savor the Flavors of Paradise:** The sweetness of tropical fruits, the delicate notes of vanilla, the freshness of poisson cru – let the island's culinary journey linger on your palate, a delicious reminder of paradise.

• **Remember the Warmth of Aloha:** Recall the genuine smiles, the friendly greetings, the helpfulness of the islanders – carry the spirit of "aloha" within you, a reminder of human connection and kindness.

Farewell, but not Goodbye

Saying goodbye to Bora Bora doesn't have to be an ending. Let it be a beginning – a wellspring of inspiration, a renewed appreciation for nature's beauty, and a reminder to embrace life with the same joy and serenity you found in paradise.

• **Keep the Dream Alive:** Share your photos and stories, inspiring others to experience the magic of Bora Bora. Let your enthusiasm keep the dream alive, both for yourself and those around you.

• **Island Home:** Decorate your space with reminders of Bora Bora – seashells, sarongs, photographs, or even recreate island-inspired dishes. Surround yourself with these mementos to keep the spirit of paradise close.

• **Plan Your Return:** Start dreaming of your next Bora Bora adventure. Research unique experiences, mark must-see attractions, and let the anticipation build for another dose of island bliss.

As you depart, remember, Bora Bora isn't just a place; it's a feeling. A feeling of serenity, connection, and appreciation for the simple beauty of life. Carry this feeling with you, let it guide your journey, and know that a part of the island's magic will forever reside within you.

A hui hou, Bora Bora. Until we meet again.

Capturing Memories:

Photography Tips

Bora Bora is a photographer's dream, with its breathtaking landscapes, vibrant colors, and unique culture. But capturing its true essence goes beyond just snapping pictures. Here are some tips to help you tell your Bora Bora story in stunning images:

• **Embrace the Golden Hour:** The magic hour before sunrise and after sunset paints the sky with mesmerizing hues. Use this time to capture dramatic silhouettes, colorful reflections, and a softer, dreamier feel to your photographs.

• **Focus on Details:** Zoom in on the intricate textures of a seashell, the delicate patterns of a flower, or the intricate carvings on a Tiki statue. These close-ups reveal the island's hidden beauty and cultural richness.

• **Capture the People:** With permission, photograph the islanders in their natural settings. Their genuine smiles, vibrant attire, and traditional activities showcase the warmth and spirit of Bora Bora's culture. Remember to be respectful and ask permission before taking their portraits.

• **Go Underwater:** Don't miss the stunning world beneath the waves! Invest in a waterproof camera or underwater housing to capture the vibrant coral reefs, playful fish, and majestic manta rays. Remember to prioritize the health of the coral and avoid touching it while taking photos.

• **Experiment with Angles:** Get creative! Climb a hill for panoramic views, lie on the beach for unique perspectives, or try underwater split-shots to showcase both the land and the sea.

• **Embrace Imperfections:** Don't strive for perfection. Capture the candid moments, the laughter lines on your face, the playful splashes in the water. These imperfections tell a story and become cherished memories.

• **Tell a Story Through Your Photos:** Don't just document, narrate! Capture interactions with locals, moments of reflection, the joy of trying new activities. Let your photos weave a captivating tale of your Bora Bora adventure.

• **Embrace the Elements:** Don't shy away from rain showers or cloudy skies. They can add a dramatic touch and showcase the island's diverse moods. Use natural light creatively to enhance your photos.

• **Edit Mindfully:** Enhance your photos, but avoid over-editing. Aim for natural color correction and subtle adjustments to bring out the best in your images.

• **Share Your Story:** Don't let your photos gather dust! Share these with your loved ones, post them on social platforms, or compile them into a photo album. Inspire others and keep the memories alive.

Remember, the best photos are those that capture the emotions and feelings you experienced in Bora Bora. So, relax, have fun, and let your camera be your canvas to paint a vibrant picture of your paradise adventure!

Made in the USA
Las Vegas, NV
08 May 2024

89715191R00069